A Field Guide to the
FROGS OF BORNEO

A Field Guide to the
FROGS OF BORNEO

Robert F. Inger and Robert B. Stuebing

Foreword by
Y.B. Datuk Tham Nyip Shen

Photographs by
C.L. Chan, A.Y.C. Chung, P. Hans Hazebroek,
M. Kottelat, Kelvin Lim, Stephen Von Peltz,
W.M. Poon, N.S. Tham, and the authors

Illustrations by
Tan Fui Lian

Natural History Publications
Kota Kinabalu

in association with

Science and Technology Unit
Sabah

1997

Published by

Natural History Publications (Borneo) Sdn. Bhd.,
A913, 9th Floor, Wisma Merdeka,
P.O. Box 13908,
88846 Kota Kinabalu, Sabah, Malaysia.
Tel: (088) 233098 Fax: (088) 240768

in association with

Science and Technology Unit,
Sabah.

First published 1997.

A Field Guide to the FROGS OF BORNEO
    by Robert F. Inger and Robert B. Stuebing

Perpustakaan Negara Malaysia Cataloguing-in-Publication Data

Inger, Robert F.
    A field guide to the frogs of Borneo / Robert F. Inger and Robert Stuebing.
    Bibliography: p. 197
    Includes Index
    ISBN 983-812-016-2
    1.Frogs—Borneo. 2. Frogs—Habitat. 3. Frog—Speciation.
    I. Stuebing, Robert. II. Title.
    597.8095983

Printed in Malaysia.

Contents

R.B. Stuebing

Foreword

There must be much pleasure on the part of specialists who have devoted years (in some cases, decades) of study of a subject to succeed in compiling an account or two of it. Frogs are no strangers to humans, yet not many of us would have come across a frog specialist. That there are now two such specialists on Bornean frogs, at least three such books and some one hundred different frogs on the island of Borneo that have received their attention is either madness, or simply proof of the fascination of these creatures.

So much abounds in the nature of Borneo that even more of such students over the next century will appear not to exhaust the topic. Yet we should find it a cause to celebrate, as specialists pause in their consuming research routines, to present their topic in a form that can be accessible to more of us. We all need to understand more about the many facets of our environment and how they interact in order to better appreciate how necessary it is to conduct our own activities carefully, with a committed intention to keep alive all these different aspects.

Herein should lie an important focus as we encourage the development of the natural sciences—the biodiversity around us is a part of our world and our science, and its study should be promoted and appreciated. As our lives change even more and there is a surge towards more "developed" societies, this respect for the diversity of life must continue.

Is not this book on frogs, as are many other forms of study of life that can reach us, a worthwhile venture of science to promote?

Tham Nyip Shen
Deputy Chief Minister and
Minister of Industrial Development,
Sabah.

P. Hans Hazebroek

Preface

It has been just under ten years since a discussion on the veranda of the Danum Valley Rest House resulted in the publication of *Frogs of Sabah*, our first attempt to introduce Bornean frogs to people outside a small circle of amphibian biologists. At the time, we were hopeful that such a book would provide a convenient window for Malaysian students, the public, and overseas visitors to have a closer look at Sabah's rich frog fauna. Happily for us, the little book seems to have succeeded at its task. But Sabah is just one fraction of Borneo. What about the frog fauna of the rest of that large island? For quite some time we did not feel up to the challenge of taking on the fauna of the whole of Borneo. Fortune has again been kind, however, and we have been able to continue working in Sabah and Sarawak, as well as receiving assistance from generous colleagues who have done field research in Kalimantan. At last we feel confident that there is sufficient information for a book with a much wider scope.

Much of the basic text of this new book is, of course, based on the original *Frogs of Sabah*. However, all of the chapters have been revised and expanded, and the coverage of species accounts increased from 56 to 97. Most Bornean frog species are covered by the key, except those for which identification is too difficult for all but a frog taxonomist. Also, since most of these species are so difficult to find that only a handful of people would ever have the opportunity to see them alive, we have restricted the colour plates in the book to cover 67% of the known frog species of Borneo. We have tried to counteract some of the difficulties of identification by providing general descriptions for most of the genera.

Complicating the task of identification for the general reader is the fact that new species continue to be discovered. In fact, 13 new species have been found since publication of *Frogs of Sabah*.

We have participated in the excitement of these discoveries and in the unravelling of the secrets in the lives of Bornean frogs. Above all, however, we have enjoyed living and working in Borneo, with people who have shown us great kindness and generosity.

Robert Inger
Robert Stuebing

W.M. Poon

CHAPTER 1

GENERAL BIOLOGY OF FROGS

Everyone can recognize a frog, which is a good indication of how distinct and relatively uniform these animals are. Their distinctive features include: (1) no tail; (2) a short, often stocky body; (3) long hind legs and short front ones; (4) large bulging eyes, and (5) a very wide mouth. Not obvious from the outside, but equally characteristic are an extraordinarily short backbone (no frog has more than nine vertebrae), virtually no ribs, and a very short digestive tract.

The long hind leg, the propulsive organ in a frog's leap, has a special, extra joint. Besides the knee and ankle connections common to all terrestrial vertebrates, frogs have another movable one across what corresponds to the middle of our foot. This extra hinge provides additional leverage for launching the body rapidly during a leap. A few frogs are not so athletic, but instead take short hops, or just walk. These unusual species, which include the Bornean Horned Frog (*Megophrys nasuta*), have rather short hind legs, but still possess the extra joint (Fig. 2).

A frog's large fleshy tongue is another organ with unusual features. It is generally very broad and soft, and unlike the tongues of birds and mammals, hinged at the front end. When feeding, a frog flips its tongue out at its prey, then flips it back in with the prey not so happily stuck on the end. That brings us to the diet, which without exception consists of animals. Insects and other invertebrates are the usual prey, though large species of frogs may devour other frogs, or even small snakes, small birds or mammals. No frog feeds on plants, though sometimes fragments

Fig. 1 (opposite). An important type of breeding site for frogs, a stream in the Maliau Basin, Sabah.

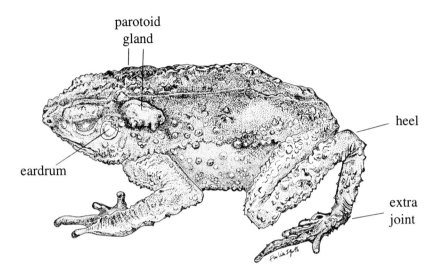

parotoid gland

heel

eardrum

extra joint

Fig. 2. Outline of frog showing anatomical features referred to in text.

of plants may be swallowed accidentally. This exclusively animal diet has resulted in a short digestive tract. In fact, generally speaking, vertebrates from fishes to mammals that feed on vegetation have long intestines, while those that feed exclusively on animals have short ones.

Another distinctive characteristic of frogs is their complex life cycle. Frogs, with few exceptions, begin life as aquatic larvae, or tadpoles (Fig. 3), and undergo a complicated series of changes called metamorphosis, as they assume the form of a frog. In general shape and way of life, hardly anything could be as different from a frog as a tadpole. Tadpoles have an egg-shaped body and a finned tail. They are truly aquatic, taking oxygen from the water by means of gills, have an extremely long, coiled intestine and feed mainly on microscopic algae and fungi. The entrance to the mouth is formed by a pair of horny beaks, while outside the mouth are rather wide lips that support rows of tiny tooth-like structures, or denticles. Most tadpoles feed by by using the lips, denticles and beaks to scrape or stir up material on the bottom, forming a small cloud of fine debris which they swallow. Elaborate structures inside the mouth are used to filter out the organic matter in the suspension that they have created.

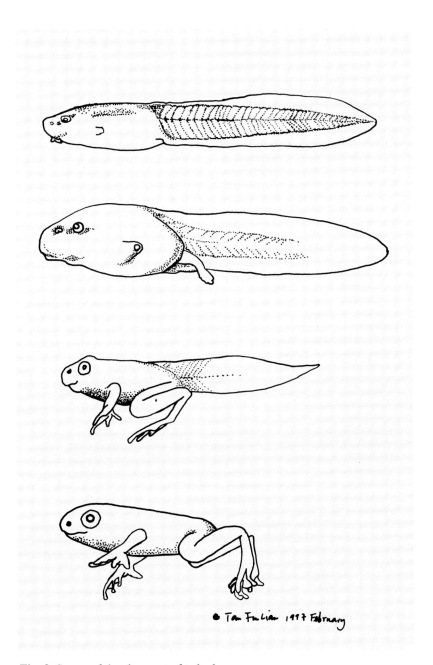

Fig. 3. Stages of development of tadpoles.

3

As they grow, their hind legs begin to develop at the end of the body. The forelimbs actually develop a bit earlier than the hind ones, but are covered by a fold of skin, and thus not visible. Some tadpoles, particularly those that live in swift flowing water, have more slender or flattened bodies and more heavily muscled tails than those living in pools of standing water. Most tadpoles have no active defenses against predators such as small fish and aquatic insects, but a few including the larvae of several Bornean frogs have poison glands that are known to make them toxic, at least to fishes.

Metamorphosis, or the change to adult body form, takes place after the limbs have fully developed, which in a few Sabah species may require only a few weeks. By that time, lungs have also developed and the tadpole is ready to breathe air. The forelimbs pop through the skin envelope, the internal gills degenerate and the tail is slowly absorbed. It is a strange process, involving many internal changes and it is hazardous for the tadpole-froglet since this odd creature is temporarily not adept at life either in the water or on land. Fortunately, metamorphosis is a rapid process, and is usually completed in a day or two.

Frogs depend on water, not just for breeding, but for basic survival. The skin of a frog is scaleless, so that water tends to pass through quite freely in either direction. Because of this characteristic of rapid permeability to water, most frogs actively avoid dryness whenever possible. Furthermore, when resting in warm, dry places (such as the forest canopy), they adopt a tight crouching posture to reduce the amount of skin exposed to the air. Interestingly, when frogs wish to drink, they rarely do so by mouth, but instead absorb water directly from a pool or other source directly through the belly skin.

Frogs occupy a wide variety of habitats. No species actually lives in the sea, although one of the frogs (*Rana cancrivora*) found in Borneo can tolerate saline waters; one was actually found swimming in the surf at the water's edge off Pulau Tiga, Sabah. In reality, frogs occur in almost all terrestrial and many aquatic environments from the cold edge of the permafrost in the far north to the to the tips of the southern continents. A few species live in deserts, more live in grasslands, but the majority live in warm, humid forests. Some species live on the ground (or under dead leaves), a few burrow in the soil, some perch on shrubs or trees at varying heights above the ground while others live in or by bodies of fresh water.

The feet and hands of most species provide clues to their habits and habitats. Frogs that live in trees and shrubs invariably have the tips of the digits enlarged into distinct pads or disks that serve as clinging devices. Many arboreal frogs have some webbing between the fingers as well as between the toes. Aquatic or ground dwelling species rarely have disks at the tips of the fingers. Aquatic and semi-aquatic frogs have extensive webbing on the feet, whereas those that burrow or live on the ground away from water usually have little webbing.

Regardless of the habitat, all but a few types of frogs lay their eggs in water, and the kind of site used for this purpose is peculiar to each species. Some frogs lay eggs in small rain pools, others in large ponds and still others in large streams or rivers. (In a later chapter we will describe the many different types of egg-laying sites used by Bornean frogs). Dependence on water for reproduction obliges many species to move relatively long distances from their usual feeding and resting sites. Although in Borneo's well watered forests the distance to a body of water cannot be very great, in drier environments such as many areas in the temperate zones, frogs have been known to migrate a kilometer or more to their breeding sites. In the case of Bornean species, reproduction can involve vertical migration as a frog moves from high in the canopy to lay eggs at a pool on the forest floor.

For most species, breeding activity begins with males at breeding sites calling, either singly or in groups. Each species has its own distinctive call. Males usually have vocal sacs in the throat which they inflate with air to form effective resonating chambers, which greatly increase the volume of the sound produced. A gravid female eventually moves towards a calling male, occasionally even bumping into him. The male climbs onto the female's back and clasps her body with his forelimbs in a behaviour called "amplexus", common to all frogs. If the pair is not in precisely the right spot, the female will move the short distance necessary while carrying the male, which in most species is the smaller of the two. As the female expels the ripe eggs into the water, the male releases his sperm and the eggs are fertilized. After a day or two, the tadpoles hatch and their aquatic life begins.

One other general feature of frogs deserves to be mentioned: the fact that most have only tiny teeth, and no claws. The Taiwanese frog, *Hoplobatrachus rugulosus*, has sharp, hard toes which can inflict minor scratches, but would be ineffective against most predators. Thus, they have rather limited defense against most predators such as snakes, birds and small mammals. Their best defense tactic is a sudden, powerful leap. For those that cannot leap, camouflage is an alternative. The Bornean Horned Frog (*Megophrys nasuta*), for example, closely resembles the dead leaves on which it sits.

A number of the frogs of Borneo have skin secretions that probably do offer some protection from predators. For example, the rufous-sided sticky frog (*Kalophrynus pleurostigma*) produces great quantities of annoyingly sticky mucous, which small predators undoubtedly find extremely unpleasant. A small snake might discover that its mouth had become glued shut after an encounter with this species. The poisonous rock frog, (*Rana hosii*) produces a skin toxin that quickly kills other frogs and can also cause serious eye irritation in humans. We suspect that a bird eating one of these frogs might never live to eat another one. The giant river toad (*Bufo juxtasper*) when disturbed secretes large amounts of a foul-smelling, toxic white latex-like substance. A dog biting one of these toads would be in serious trouble. So, as a simple precaution, it is always wise to wash hands thoroughly after handling any frog.

CHAPTER 2

FROGS IN HUMAN TRADITION AND CULTURE

Despite a diversity of nearly 150 species in Borneo, frogs do not play a particularly prominent role in the folklore and traditions of the many human cultures of the island. The evidence for this lies mainly in the number of names given: birds, for example, feature prominently in the culture of the Iban people of western Borneo, so that a wide variety of species have individual names. Among the coastal peoples such as the Malays, Bajau and others, literally hundreds of different names distinguish individual members of a great diversity of marine and estuarine life, primarily for the purpose of designating food from non-food, and dangerous from harmless species. Since frogs are neither conspicuous (like birds) nor a staple food item (such as fish or prawns), stories about them tend to be limited to minor folk tales, and uses of them to a few home remedies, or minor additions to the diet.

Though people in Borneo are rather knowledgeable about the natural history of frogs in general, they often pay them little attention. There is an old belief from inland Sabah that a frog that bites will not release its grip until there is the sound of thunder (similar to a belief about *Chelydra serpentina*, the common snapping turtle in the USA). Despite the fact that the giant river frog, *Rana leporina*, and some related species possess fang-like projections on the lower jaw, few people in Borneo believe a frog would ever bite in the first place. The "fangs", incidentally, are used in courtship battles, *e.g.*, only between members of the same species. As far as snapping at objects, only prey-sized ones (mostly insects) are targets, and no frog has yet been found quite large enough to snap up a man. There is, in fact, a rather pointed, philosophical saying in Malay, "to die from the nip of a frog", which in context means that a proud or important character can be brought low by a small, insignificant person or event.

To a large measure in Bornean culture, frogs personify anything from timidity to small-mindedness, amongst other things. Lack of resolve is seen in the way frogs flee, panic-stricken, from a snake. A provincial person is described, appropriately, as "a frog under a coconut shell", while someone who is out of his depth is said to be like "a frog caught by a drought". Those who are overly optimistic are likened to frogs who "celebrate at the mere hint of rain", and if they aspire to things that far exceed their abilities, they are "like a frog who wants to be (as big as a) bull". The English saying that a leopard cannot change his spots is instead rendered, "a toad will never have smooth skin no matter how much it rains". Finally, to die in a manner that leaves no hope of survival is "to die like a frog".

Many people in Malaysian Borneo will remark that frogs can call the rain, and this notion is not without foundation. Though the frogs obviously do not bring rain, many species, including horned frogs (*Megophrys nasuta*) and sticky frogs (*Kaloula* spp.) certainly sense the decrease in barometric pressure that precedes a heavy rain storm. In Danum Valley, Sabah, a chorus of horned frogs frequently bursts forth a few minutes in advance of a thunderstorm. A sticky frog (*Kaloula pulchra*) was heard immediately prior to a storm on Gaya Island, near Kota Kinabalu. The hypnotic influence of rain on frogs in general is used to describe persons who are daydreaming or dazed, who are said to have the same blank stare as "a frog sitting under a spray of water".

Though frogs are rarely regarded as mysterious or hazardous, some taboos or "berkenan" are associated with them. Pregnant women are not to look upon certain creatures, for fear the latter will influence the traits of her unborn child. Similarly, a man whose wife is pregnant should not kill certain animals, for the same reason given above. These animals, including frogs, reputedly have power to influence the unborn, so that the offspring of a man who during his wife's pregnancy has killed a frog, may have an offspring born to look like one.

In the folklore of the Dusun people of the Mount Kinabalu area, a story is told of a hunter and a giant frog. (The story was related by Mr. Ansow Gunsalam of Kinabalu Park).

"Many years ago, a man living in a village near Mount Kinabalu went out hunting, but it soon rained so heavily that he was forced to take shelter

beneath an overhanging rock. He soon felt a chill, so he lit himself a fire and began to cook a meal. Suddenly there was a rumbling sound, followed by a landslide, and when he looked up he was terrified to find that the overhanging boulder under which he had taken shelter was actually a huge frog, covered with moss. The men fled for his life, but on his way home had the good fortune to capture a young monkey, and thus did not return empty-handed.

When he returned, he found a marriage celebration was well underway, with many people already drunk on rice wine (tapai) while they beat the gongs and danced the sumazau. Amazingly, to the delight of all, the monkey began to dance around as well. In fun, the drunken men dressed him up in childrens' clothes, pairing him with a similarly dressed cat, and urging him to dance some more. The noise of the gongs grew louder and louder, and everyone laughed hilariously. The bride, however, was not amused, and went for water at the well nearby. When she looked in to take water, she was shocked to find a giant frog sitting inside, and even more stunned when he told her to take her husband and seek to escape the place, for disaster was imminent.

Only moments after the bride and groom took to their heels in terror, a huge flood appeared from nowhere and engulfed the revelers, abruptly silencing the peals of laughter and the booming of the gongs. Afterwards, when survivors dug for the bodies of the victims, they found only dead frogs. Thus, to this day the local people warn their children never do laugh at animals, for fear of great misfortune."

Knowledge that the skin of toads is highly toxic seems almost universal. In fact, some old Malay charms for revenge do make use of toad skin in the prescribed mixture. Nevertheless, although Muslim Malays and others never eat frogs, toads and their larvae are eaten by a number of the other traditional peoples of Borneo. In Sabah, Kadazan-Dusuns fry tadpoles (of any species) as a gourmet delight, while in Sarawak, the Bidayuh people cook them with fermented durian paste (*tempoyak*). For adult toads, however, the Kadazan-Dusuns, Ibans, Bidayuhs and others are always careful to remove the skin before dining on the meat. Some people also avoid eating the bones of a toad, which are regarded as poisonous.

The species of frogs most sought-after for the table include the *Rana leporina* group ("S'ai" in Dusun, "pamak" in Iban) , which includes *R.*

ingeri, *R. malesiana* and *R. ibanorum*. Most are forest frogs which grow to a length of about 10–15 cm and have heavily muscled legs. In coastal areas, the crab-eating frog of mangrove, *Rana cancrivora*, is the frog of choice, and served up in Chinese restaurants as "theen kai" or "paddy chicken". In Sabah, an exotic species called "bongkok Taiwan" or Taiwanese frog (*Hoplobatrachus rugulosus*) was introduced, probably in the 1960s. It has since become widespread throughout disturbed habitats all over the State, and has become a popular source of frog's legs for the table. Since it grows to nearly three times the size of the mangrove frog, its popularity has grown to the extent that in order to purchase the meat in some local *tamu*, or markets, a person must be on the spot before 5.00 a.m., since the supply can easily be sold out by six. More recently in large towns such as Kuching and Kota Kinabalu, farming of the American Bullfrog has been underway for a few years and has begun to supply most of the local demand for frogs. Since the above species is larger and meatier than any Bornean species (even *Rana blythi*), exploitation of the latter, at least in the major towns, is likely to decline.

The most common way frogs are prepared locally is to fry them either in batter (Fig. 4) or with ginger and *tau gey* (bean sprouts), though people of the interior swear that boiling the frogs without removing the skin provides a meal fit for a king. Indeed, chicken comes out second best to the fine and delicate flavor of frog meat for those of us willing to forget the latter's humble origins.

Fig. 4. Plate of frogs' leg fried in batter.

CHAPTER 3

DISTRIBUTION AND CLASSIFICATION OF FROGS OF BORNEO

At least 140 species of frogs occur in Borneo. The exact number is uncertain because new species are discovered every year. Thirty years ago when the first comprehensive review of the frogs of Borneo was published there were only 92 species on the list. Thirteen completely new species have been discovered since 1990. We cannot guess how many more remain to be found, but the total number will undoubtedly top 150.

These frogs belong to six families: Bombinatoridae, Megophryidae, Bufonidae (the so-called "true toads"), Microhylidae, Ranidae (the so-called "true frogs"), and Rhacophoridae. Except for the Bombinatoridae, these families are widely distributed in Southeast Asia. There are no good common names for these families; "true frogs" and "true toads" only mean that the few species found in England belong to these families, which is surely a strange definition of "true."

The amphibian order to which the frogs belong (the Anura) has existed for at least two hundred million years, the oldest identifiable frog fossil having been found in rocks of that age. The most widely held opinion on the evolution of frogs places the families Ranidae and Rhacophoridae (sometimes called the Oriental tree frogs) close together, although their separation goes back at least 75 million years. The Microhylidae (often called narrow-mouthed frogs) are considered to be an earlier offshoot of the same line. The other three families represent quite distinct and separate lines of evolution.

Each of the Bornean families is divided into groups of related species or genera ("genus" is the singular). There are 31 genera, but the species are not evenly divided among them. Four of the genera contain almost 40% of the species and eleven of them have only a single Bornean species. (See the checklist at the end of this chapter.) Some of the genera containing a single species probably represent peculiar evolutionary pathways—species that have developed peculiar anatomical features adapted for an unusual way of life. On the other hand, the genera with many species seem to be examples of body plans that have been broadly successful in a variety of habitats.

In some of the larger genera, certain species seem to form related groups if we examine anatomy of adults and tadpoles and their behaviour. Within the genus *Rana*, the two guardian frogs, *Rana palavanensis* and *R. finchi*, constitute a distinctive species group characterized by reduced webbing and, most remarkably, the habit of males to guard the eggs and then transport the tadpoles to water. In fact, these two frogs are so similar that they were once thought to be races of a single species.

Tree frogs of the genus *Rhacophorus* form several groups of related species. The medium-sized to large species having fully webbed fingers, Wallace's Flying Frog (*Rhacophorus nigropalmatus*), Reinwardt's Flying Frog (*R. reinwardtii*), the Harlequin Tree Frog (*R. pardalis*), and the Jade Tree Frog (*R. dulitensis*), all have smooth-edged flaps of skin along the outer edge of the fore arms, all have the ability to parachute or glide, and all have large tadpoles that live in small pools of standing water. Three small tree frogs, *Rhacophorus angulirostris, R. bimaculatus*, and *R. gauni* constitute another group. These small species have only partially webbed fingers and have a pointed projection of skin near the heel. Their tadpoles live in small, clear, rocky-bottomed streams.

Generally, taxonomists arrange species into groups based on their shared characteristics. Once that is done, patterns of evolution and relationships become more apparent. Those patterns, in turn, may enable us to predict the behaviour and life-cycles of frogs we may have identified but whose habits we know little about.

The geographic distribution of this large Bornean fauna fits clear patterns. The most striking thing about it is that it is different from any other fauna in the general region. Almost two-thirds of the species (63%

or 89 species) have never been found outside of Borneo. Fifteen of these have been seen only once, so it is no surprise that they are not known from anywhere else. But most of the Borneo "endemics" (as species confined to one area are called) have been found many times—for example, the Dwarf Litter Frog (*Leptobrachella mjöbergi*) and the Marbled Tree Toad (*Pedostibes rugosus*). Perhaps more collecting in adjacent lands—Peninsular Malaysia, Sumatra, or the Philippines—may turn up some of the Bornean endemics, but it is not likely to affect the general picture: the Bornean frog fauna is mainly unique to the island. This uniqueness implies that some groups have been isolated from the rest of Southeast Asia for many millions of years.

Nevertheless, Borneo's fauna does show links to adjacent areas. Thirty nine Bornean species have been recorded in Peninsular Malaysia, 32 species also occur in Sumatra, and 18 species are also found in the Philippine Islands. Twenty five species are known from Thailand, and a few Bornean species occur throughout much of Southeast Asia. This situation is not surprising since these connections are consequences of past geological history, geographical proximity, and similar vegetation and climate. Bornean snakes, birds, mammals, and freshwater fishes show the same kinds of relationships to the faunas of adjacent lands.

Earlier in this chapter we noted that one family, the Bombinatoridae, is not widespread in Southeast Asia. In fact, the genus to which the Bornean species belongs, *Barbourula*, is known from just two species, the Bornean species (known from a single locality in Kalimantan) and one from Palawan and two small islands in the Philippines just north of Sabah. The nearest family relative occurs in northern Vietnam and southern China.

The statement that a particular species occurs in Borneo should not be understood to imply that the species has been found throughout the island. In fact, not much is known about the distribution of frogs in Kalimantan, the largest portion of Borneo, because so little collecting has been done there. Nonetheless, enough work has been done to enable us to see some patterns. What appears to be true is that there are not major differences among large parts of Borneo. Most of the species living in hilly terrain of the lowland rain forest seem to occur throughout Borneo. For example, the Giant River Frog (*Rana leporina*) has been found wherever the frog fauna has been sampled below 600 metres above sea level, except in peat swamp forests. The Rock Skipper (*Staurois latopalmatus*) is known from every part of Borneo that has rocky streams with swift currents. However, there are a few lowland species that seem to be restricted to certain regions. For example, the Rough Guardian Frog (*Rana finchi*) has been found only in Sabah so far, despite intensive sampling throughout Sarawak; we suspect that it also occurs in the eastern parts of Kalimantan. The Rough-Backed River Frog (*Rana ibanorum*) has been found in many places in Kalimantan, Sarawak, and Brunei, but has yet to be discovered in Sabah.

The frog species that live only in montane forest (higher than 1000 metres above sea level) have restricted regional distributions in Borneo, simply because montane environments do not exist throughout the island. At one time, it was thought that many of the species found originally on Mount Kinabalu were found nowhere else, but that has been shown to be untrue as a result of recent exploration of high elevations on Mount Trus Madi and Mount Lumaku in Sabah, and on Mount Mulu in northern Sarawak. Unfortunately little is yet known of the frogs living above 1000 metres in montane parts of Kalimantan. there is certainly potential for many new discoveries in this vast southern and eastern part of Borneo.

R.B. Stuebing

Fig. 5. Recently emerged froglet of Reinwardt's Flying Frog (*Rhacophorus reinwardtii*).

KEY TO FROGS OF BORNEO

1 Conspicuous webbing on hand, at least between two outer fingers 2
   No webbing between outer fingers 17

2 Webbing between fingers thick, fleshy .... *Pelophryne*[1]
   Webbing between fingers thin, membranous 3

3 Colour black with irregular, small light spots or lines ....
   .... *Staurois latopalmatus*
   Body not black 4

4 Top of head and sides extremely rough and warty ....
   .... *Theloderma horridum*
   Not as above 5

5 Body green 6
   Body not green 8

6 Adults less than 25 mm, snout pointed and webbing limited to base of
   fingers .... *Rhacophorus kajau*
   Adults more than 25 mm 7

7 Sides black, with blue and golden yellow spots ....
   .... *Rhacophorus reinwardti*
   Sides yellowish or greenish .... *Rhacophorus nigropalmatus*

8 Webbing red 9
   Webbing not red 10

9 Forearm with flap of skin along outer edge .... *Rhacophorus pardalis*
   Forearm with no skin flap .... *Rhacophorus rufipes*

10 Heel with conspicuous pointed projection of skin ....
   .... *Rhacophorus baluensis*
   No such projection 11

11 Outer edge of lower leg with row of pointed projections or frill of skin
   12
   Outer edge of lower leg otherwise 13

12 Top of head and back with spiky projections .... *Rhacophorus everetti*

---

1) *Pelophryne* are small toads (usually less than 25 mm). Even so-called experts find it difficult to separate the species.

Top of head without spiky projections ..... *Rhacophorus appendiculatus*

13   Pale blue spots on sides, groin and inner thigh ....
.... *Rhacophorus bimaculatus*
Sides and thigh without blue spots 14

14   Small (less than 40 mm) frog with short, blunt snout, and a white spot
under the eye .... *Rhacophorus gauni*
Not as above 15

15   Sides yellowish with black spots .... *Rhacophorus angulirostris*
Not as above 16

16   Snout sharp, with conspicuous sharp ridge between eye and nostril
.... *Rhacophorus harrissoni*
Snout blunt, without sharp ridge .... *Rhacophorus fasciatus*

17   A large conspicuous "wart" or gland (parotoid gland) behind eye in
shoulder area, as large as or larger than the eye 18
No large gland behind eye 24

18   Top of head between eyes with a pair of narrow, raised ridges 19
Without such ridges 20

19   Parotoid gland narrow and elongated .... *Bufo quadriporcatus*
Parotoid oval or triangular .... *Bufo divergens*

20   Tips of fingers flattened and squarish in outline 21
Tips of fingers rounded or tapered 22

21   Parotoid gland rounded; body green with brown or reddish spots ....
.... *Pedostibes rugosus*
Parotoid gland elongated, narrow; body brown or black with irregular
yellow lines .... *Pedostibes hosii*

22   A bony ridge curving around eye to parotoid gland ....
.... *Bufo melanostictus*
Without such a ridge 23

23   Parotoid gland round or slightly oval, about the size of the eye ....
.... *Bufo asper*
Parotoid elongated, much longer than the eye .... *Bufo juxtasper*

24   Conspicuous projection of skin from surface of upper eyelid 25
No such projection 27

2) *Megophrys baluensis* is so far known only from Mount Kinabalu and has short legs similar to *M. nasuta*. *Megophrys dringi* has so far been found only on Mount Mulu and is a long-legged species.
3) Species of *Calluella* are burrowers and rarely encountered. Distinctions among them are discussed in the text.
4) These tiny species are rarely seen and can be distinguished from each other only with the aid of a microscope.
5) To see this feature it is necessary to gently pry the mouth of the frog open.

Tip of lower jaw with several cusps 37

36 Chest and abdomen whitish, without spots .... *Occidozyga laevis*
    Chest and abdomen with many dark spots .... *Occidozyga baluensis*

37 All toes webbed to tips .... *Rana kuhlii*
    Toes not fully webbed .... *Rana laticeps*

38 Fourth or outer finger less than half the length of the first finger 39
    Fourth finger almost as long or longer than the first finger 41

39 Spots present in the groin area 40
    No spots in the groin .... *Kalophrynus* spp.[6]

40 Spots bluish or whitish .... *Kalophrynus heterochirus*
    Spot(s) black .... *Kalophrynus pleurostigma*

41 Eardrum sunken, within a cavity .... *Huia cavitympanum*
    Eardrum not as above 42

42 Back cinnamon-coloured or red, speckled with white; a white spot on
    the upper eyelid .... *Nyctixalus pictus*
    Colouration not as above 43

43 Top of first two toes white or blue 44
    Toes not as above 45

44 Top of head and body with dark to black spots on a greenish
    background .... *Staurois natator*
    Top of head and body dark green to blackish with a few small light
    spots .... *Staurois tuberilinguis*

45 Underside of fingers with enlarged pads, broader than the finger tips;
    tree hole frog .... *Metaphrynella sundana*
    Fingers without such pads 46

46 Belly golden yellow with black network .... *Chaperina fusca*
    Belly not as above 47

47 Back chocolate brown bodered by a thin pale blue or whitish line, sides
    gray to black .... *Rana luctuosa*
    Colouration otherwise 48

---

6) Several small species of this genus are extremely difficult to separate. See descriptions in text.

48 Body green with a light yellowish stripe down each side of the back
.... *Rana erythraea*
Colouration otherwise 49

49 Body dark brown or black, with yellowish or reddish spots, always with
light edge to upper eyelid 50
Colouration otherwise 51

50 A continuous yellowish or orange stripe on each side of back from eye
to end of body .... *Rana signata*
Yellow or orange spots on back never forming continuous stripe ....
.... *Rana picturata*

51 Body green, usually without spots; upper lip white 52
Body usually not green; if green, lip not white 53

52 Fourth toe (the longest) with at least two joints free of web; underside
of thigh usually reddish .... *Rana chalconota*
Fourth toe with web reaching base of expanded tip; underside of thigh
never reddish .... *Rana hosii*

53 Fourth toe (the longest) fully webbed to base of tip 54
Fourth toe with at least two joints free of full web 58

54 A series of short ridges down the back; throat always with dark pattern
.... 55
Back without many short ridges; throat may have dark pattern 56

55 Throat with dark streak down centre; back always with black spots
.... *Hoplobatrachus rugulosus*
Throat without dark central streak; back usually without visible spotting
.... *Rana ibanorum*

56 Entire upper surface covered with low, rounded warts ....
.... *Pseudobufo subasper*
Upper surface with some tubercles and ridges, but not completely rough
.... 57

57 A dark stripe between eye and nostril on side of snout; top and side of
snout form a sharp angle .... *Rana leporina*
No dark stripe on side of snout; a rounded surface formed by top and
side of snout .... *Rana ingeri*

58 Toes not webbed 59
Toes at least partially webbed 64

19

---

7) The small species in this genus are difficult to separate from one another without a microscope. See descriptions in text.
8) Taxonomists are still trying to sort out the species of this genus and in the process new species are being discovered steadily. See descriptions in text.

.... *Ansonia latidisca*[9]

Tips of fingers not wider than last joint 71

71 A white or cream-coloured streak from eye to armpit ....
.... *Ansonia albomaculata*

Without such a streak 72

72 Third and fifth toes webbed to tips .... *Ansonia guibei*

Third and fifth toes not webbed to tips .... *Ansonia* spp.[10]

73 A series of short ridges on the back 74

A few rounded rough areas or back smooth 75

74 Three joints of the fourth toe (the longest) with no webbing ....
.... *Rana limnocharis*

Only one or two joints of fourth toe without webbing ....
.... *Rana cancrivora*

75 A dark streak from eye to nostril on side of snout; usually entire eardrum covered by large dark marking; head narrow ....
.... *Rana paramacrodon*

No dark streak from eye to nostril; usually about half of eardrum covered by dark pigment; head wide .... *Rana malesiana*

76 Head narrow, snout long, distance between eye and nostril longer than eye diameter .... *Rana nicobariensis*

Head wider, snout shorter, diameter of eye longer than distance between eye and nostril 77

77 A conspicuous saw-edged bony ridge above the eardrum ....
.... *Polypedates otilophus*

No such ridge 78

78 Eardrum covered by dark band extending along shoulder to armpit
.... *Polypedates macrotis*

Pattern otherwise 79

79 Outer toe webbed to base of pad 80

Outer toe not webbed to pad 82

---

9) Distinguishing among these three is a task for taxonomists. The first two do not occur below 900 metres above sea level.

10) Four species of *Ansonia* that are difficult to separate share this characteristic. See descriptions in text.

80 Third toe webbed to base of pad on both sides 81
    Third toe not webbed to pad on both sides .... *Philautus hosii*
    .... *Philautus ingeri*[11]

81 Back and sides bright green with dark spots ....
    .... *Meristogenys kinabaluensis*
    Back and sides brown or black .... *Meristogenys* spp.[12]

82 Tips of fingers not much wider than next joint 83
    Tips of fingers about twice width of next joint 84

83 Sides with enlarged skin glands, producing a rough or pebbled surface
    .... *Rana glandulosa*
    Skin of side not as above .... *Rana baramica*

84 Pad of longest finger about same width as eardrum .... *Philautus* spp.[13]
    Pad of longest finger much narrower than eardrum 85

85 Legs rather short; skin rough .... *Ingerana baluensis*
    Legs long; skin smooth 86

86 Snout sharply pointed .... *Polypedates collettii*
    Snout not pointed .... *Polypedates leucomystax*

---

11) *Philautus hosii* is confined to elevations below 750 metres and *P. ingeri* to elevations above 1000 metres.

12) The remainder of the species in this genus are difficult to separate even for taxonomists. Consult descriptions in text.

13) These small species (usually less than 25 mm) pose serious problems even for herpetologists. See descriptions in text.

A Checklist of Anuran Amphibians currently known from Borneo

Family Bombinatoridae

1   *Barbourula kalimantanensis* Iskandar *

Family Megophryidae

2   *Leptobrachella baluensis* Smith *
3   *L. brevicrus* Dring *
4   *L. mjöbergi* Smith *
5   *L. parva* Dring *
6   *L. palmata* Inger & Stuebing *
7   *L. serasanae* Dring *
8   *Leptobrachium abbotti* (Cochran) *
9   *L. hendricksoni* Taylor
10   *L. montanum* Fischer *
11   *L. nigrops* Berry & Hendrickson
12   *Leptolalax dringi* Dubois *
13   *L. gracilis* (Günther)
14   *L. hamidi* Matsui *
15   *L. maura* Inger, Maklarin, Alim & Yambun *
16   *L. pictus* Malkmus *
17   *Megophrys baluensis* (Boulenger) *
18   *M. dringi* Inger, Stuebing & Tan *
19   *M. edwardinae* Inger *
20   *M. nasuta* (Schlegel)

Family Bufonidae

21   *Ansonia albomaculata* Inger *
22   *A. fuliginea* (Mocquard) *
23   *A. guibei* Inger *
24   *A. hanitschi* Inger *
25   *A. latidisca* Inger *
26   *A. leptopus* (Günther) *
27   *A. longidigita* Inger *
28   *A. minuta* Inger *
29   *A. platysoma* Inger *
30   *A. spinulifer* (Mocquard) *
31   *A. torrentis* Dring *

32 *Bufo asper* Gravenhorst
33 *B. divergens* Peters *
34 *B. juxtasper* Inger *
35 *B. melanostictus* Schneider
36 *B. quadriporcatus* Boulenger
37 *Leptophryne borbonica* (Tschudi)
38 *Pedostibes everetti* (Boulenger) *
39 *P. hosii* (Boulenger) *
40 *P. maculatus* (Mocquard) *
41 *P. rugosus* Inger *
42 *Pelophryne api* Dring *
43 *P. brevipes* (Peters)
44 *P. exigua* (Boettger)
45 *P. guentheri* (Boulenger) *
46 *P. macrotis* (Boulenger) *
47 *P. misera* (Mocquard) *
48 *P. rhopophilius* Inger & Stuebing *
49 *Pseudobufo subasper* Tschudi

Family Microhylidae
50 *Calluella brooksi* (Boulenger) *
51 *C. flava* Kiew *
52 *C. smithi* (Barbour & Noble) *
53 *Chaperina fusca* Mocquard
54 *Gastrophrynoides borneensis* (Boulenger) *
55 *Kalophrynus baluensis* Kiew *
56 *K. heterochirus* Boulenger *
57 *K. intermedius* Inger *
58 *K. nubicola* Dring *
59 *K. pleurostigma* (Tschudi)
60 *K. punctatus* Peters *
61 *K. subterrestris* Inger *
62 *Kaloula baleata* (Müller)
63 *K. pulchra* Gray
64 *Metaphrynella sundana* (Peters)
65 *Microhyla berdmorei* (Blyth)
66 *M. borneensis* Parker *
67 *M. maculifera* Inger *
68 *M. perparva* Inger & Frogner *
69 *M. petrigena* Inger & Frogner *

Family Ranidae

70   *Hoplobatrachus rugulosa* (Wiegmann)
71   *Huia cavitympanum* (Boulenger) *
72   *Ingerana baluensis* (Boulenger) *
73   *Meristogenys amoropalamus* (Matsui) *
74   *M. jerboa* (Günther) *
75   *M. kinabaluensis* (Inger) *
76   *M. macrophthalmus* (Matsui) *
77   *M. orphnocnemis* (Matsui) *
78   *M. phaeomerus* (Inger & Gritis) *
79   *M. poecilus* (Inger & Gritis) *
80   *M. whiteheadi* (Boulenger) *
81   *Occidozyga baluensis* (Boulenger) *
82   *O. laevis* (Günther)
83   *Rana asperata* Inger, Boeadi & Taufik *
84   *R. baramica* Boettger
85   *R. cancrivora* (Gravenhorst)
86   *R. chalconota* (Schlegel)
87   *R. erythraea* (Schlegel)
88   *R. finchi* Inger *
89   *R. glandulosa* Boulenger
90   *R. hosii* Boulenger
91   *R. ibanorum* Inger *
92   *R. ingeri* Kiew *
93   *R. kenepaiensis* Inger *
94   *R. kuhlii* Tschudi
95   *R. laticeps* Boulenger
96   *R. leporina* Andersson *
97   *R. limnocharis* Boie
98   *R. luctuosa* (Peters)
99   *R. malesiana* Kiew
100   *R. nicobariensis* (Stoliczka)
101   *R. palavanensis* Boulenger
102   *R. paramacrodon* Inger *
103   *R. picturata* Boulenger *
104   *R. rhacoda* Inger, Boeadi & Taufik *
105   *R. signata* (Günther)
106   *Staurois latopalmatus* (Boulenger) *
107   *S. natator* (Günther) *
108   *S. tuberilinguis* Boulenger *

Family Rhacophoridae

109 *Nyctixalus pictus* (Peters)
110 *Philautus acutus* Dring *
111 *P. amoenus* Smith *
112 *P. aurantium* Inger *
113 *P. bunitus* Inger, Stuebing & Tan *
114 *P. disgregus* Inger *
115 *P. hosii* (Boulenger) *
116 *P. ingeri* Dring *
117 *P. kerangae* Dring *
118 *P. longicrus* (Boulenger) *
119 *P. mjöbergi* Smith *
120 *P. petersi* (Boulenger) *
121 *P. refugii* Inger & Stuebing *
122 *P. tectus* Dring *
123 *P. umbra* Dring *
124 *Polypedates colletti* (Boulenger)
125 *P. leucomystax* (Gravenhorst)
126 *P. macrotis* (Boulenger)
127 *P. otilophus* (Boulenger) *
128 *Rhacophorus angulirostris* Ahl *
129 *R. appendiculatus* (Günther)
130 *R. baluensis* Inger *
131 *R. bimaculatus* (Peters)
132 *R. dulitensis* Boulenger *
133 *R. everetti* Boulenger *
134 *R. fasciatus* Boulenger
135 *R. gauni* (Inger) *
136 *R. harrissoni* Inger & Haile *
137 *R. kajau* Dring *
138 *R. nigropalmatus* Boulenger
139 *R. pardalis* Günther
140 *R. reinwardtii* (Schlegel)
141 *R. rufipes* Inger *
142 *Theloderma horridum* (Boulenger)

* Species endemic to the island of Borneo.

CHAPTER 4

ECOLOGY OF BORNEAN FROGS

There are two major groups of frogs in Borneo based on their general habits and habitats. The smaller of the two groups consists of species closely associated with human economic activity, frogs that live in padi fields or other types of cultivation, kampungs, towns or city habitats such as drainage ditches, or vegetation around buildings. Nine species fall into this category: the Taiwanese Frog (*Hoplobatrachus rugulosus*), Green Paddy Frog (*Rana erythraea*), Mangrove Frog (*Rana cancrivora*), Grass Frog (*Rana limnocharis*), Cricket Frog (*Rana nicobariensis*), Black-spotted Toad (*Bufo melanostictus*), Four-lined Tree Frog (*Polypedates leucomystax*), Banded Bullfrog (*Kaloula pulchra*) and Brown Bullfrog (*Kaloula baleata*). Not only do these species live close to humans; they even depend on us to create favorable environmental conditions such as puddles, ponds (Fig. 6), and ditches within large open, disturbed areas. Only *Rana nicobariensis* and *Polypedates leucomystax* can be found in secondary growth or near primary forest. All of the nine species breed in standing water: drains, ornamental pools, temporary rain-filled depressions and flooded rice fields. Only one species is a real climber, *Polypedates leucomystax*, which perches on tall grasses and scrubby vegetation, though *Rana erythraea* males are known to perch in low bushes in some instances. Two species are burrowers, the sticky bullfrogs, *Kaloula pulchra* and *Kaloula baleata* and the former is frequently found among the dead leaves clogging a drain which is in the process of being cleaned. *Rana erythraea* and *Rana cancrivora* rarely move more than a few metres from water, whereas *Rana limnocharis* and *Rana nicobariensis* are great travelers, moving through damp grass and shrubbery often at some distance from water.

Many or perhaps most of these "town" or kampung" species arrived in Borneo as stowaways, inadvertently brought in by human travelers. Both *Kaloula pulchra* and *Hoplobatrachus rugulosus* appeared relatively recently in Sabah, and the latter has not yet found its way to Sarawak. *Bufo melanosticus* is common in Sarawak, but so far found only in one kampung (village) in Sabah (near Kampung Kibunut, in the West Coast), indicating that it is still slowly spreading. *Hoplobatrachus rugulosus*, or "Bongkok Taiwan", was introduced in Sabah as a source of food perhaps as early as the 1970s (See Chapter 2).

Fig. 6. Pond with frogs.

The great majority of Bornean frogs are confined either to forests or to forest edges. One or two species, such as the Saffron-bellied Frog (*Chaperina fusca*), occasionally make a go of it in shady gardens. Generally, however, the vast majority of frogs in Borneo are forest dwellers, and take up one of the following life-styles:

(1)   Some frogs never leave the banks of streams. Their tadpoles always develop in those streams (Fig. 7) or rivers, and when the newly transformed froglets emerge from the water, they stay in the vicinity where they feed and grow—if they can avoid predators such as other frogs, snakes or lizards. Frogs of this type include the Giant River Frog (*Rana leporina*), Kuhl's Creek Frog (*Rana kuhlii*), the Giant River Toad (*Bufo juxtasper*) and the Black-spotted Rock Frog (*Staurois natator*).

28

Frogs of wetland areas should also be included, ones such as the Greater Swamp Frog (*Rana ingeri*) and the Yellow-bellied Puddle Frog (*Occidozyga laevis*).

(2)   Certain species of frogs commonly found along the banks of streams live away from the water during their juvenile or pre-reproductive stage. The Spotted Stream Frog, *Rana picturata* and its close relative, *Rana signata*, as well as the poisonous Rock Frog, *Rana hosei*, are good examples. Tadpoles develop in quiet areas of small streams, often in brown masses or accumulations of rotting vegetation called "leaf drifts". When the larvae metamorphose into tiny froglets about a centimeter in length, these juveniles hop away into the forest, sometimes as far as several hundred metres from the water. There, again if they can avoid numerous predators, they will feed and grow to about 2.5 cm long. After reaching this stage, they will return to their stream, where they will breed and remain for the duration of their lives.

R.F. Inger

Fig. 7. Stream in hilly lowland forest.

(3)   A third group of species uses streams only for breeding. Typically, one of these frogs (for example, the Brown Tree Toad, *Pedostibes hosei*) emerges as a tiny toadlet from the side pool of a stream and hops away into the forest, to live there for the rest of its life, returning to the stream only at intervals, to breed. Numerous frogs in Borneo display this life style, including the famous horned frogs (*Megophrys* spp.), the litter frogs (*Leptobrachium* spp.), the White-lipped Frog (*Rana chalconota*) and the Harlequin Tree Frog (*Rhacophorus pardalis*), among others.

(4)   Many of the frogs of Borneo spend their lives wandering widely through the forest, and are rarely encountered along the banks of streams. The majority of these species forage within the forest floor litter (Fig. 8). Most of them lay their eggs in small pools on the forest floor (Fig. 9), while some use water-filled tree-holes and others deposit their eggs within the leaf litter where there may be no standing water, but where the humidity is high and stable. Forest pools can be formed in cavities created by uprooted trees, or by large animals such as wild pigs (or in earlier times, the rhinoceros) that excavate wallows in areas of soft

R.F. Inger

Fig. 8 (above). Searching through leaf litter for frogs in lowland forest.
Fig. 9 (opposite). Pool in lowland forest, breeding site of many frogs.

mud. Canopy-dwelling frogs such as Wallace's Flying Frog (*Rhacophorus nigropalmatus*), Reinwardt's Flying Frog (*Rhacophorus reinwardtii*) and others, descend to hang their foam nests at the edge of these pools, usually attaching the frothy egg mass to overhanging vegetation (Fig. 10). Terrestrial forest species such as the Saffron-bellied Frog (*Chaperina fusca*) or the Mahogany Frog (*Rana luctuosa*) also breed in such pools.

Arboreal, or tree-living frogs that breed in water-containing tree holes seem to recognize the difference between large and small trees. The tiny, Piping Tree-hole Frog (*Metaphrynella sundana*) seeks out holes in trees or lianas that have trunks or stems no larger than about 12 cm. In contrast, the Cinnamon Tree Frog (*Nyctixalus pictus*) always deposits its eggs in holes located in trees having a trunk diameter always larger than

R.B. Stuebing

Fig. 10. Foam nest of tree frog overhanging rhino wallow.

about 30 cm. The Brown Tree Frog (*Rhacophorus harrissoni*) uses not only holes in the trunks of large trees for breeding, but deposits its eggs even in the "troughs" formed by fused buttress roots of giant mengaris ("tapang") trees (*Koompassia excelsa*).

Several of the species of bush frogs (genus *Philautus*) lay a reduced number of eggs, from 6–12, under dead leaves, or beneath dead logs or layers of damp moss. The larva develops in an unusual way, undergoing the process of development within the egg, not as a tadpole, but as a tiny froglet with a tail. The froglet remains within the egg until all internal organs typical of an adult frog have formed. Frogs of this type clearly have acquired a life cycle that is completely independent of bodies of water. They succeed especially well in high altitude or montane forests where a blanket of wet, spongy moss covers many exposed surfaces.

Types of life cycles have little to do with a frog's vertical or foraging zone in the forest. There are arboreal and terrestrial species in each of these types of life cycles. Frogs living on the ground use a variety of microhabitats or substrates: the Greater Swamp Frog (*Rana ingeri*) usually sits on mud, whereas its larger relative, the Giant River Frog (*Rana leporina*) most frequently is found on gravel or sand. The Rock Skipper (*Staurois latopalmatus*) emerges at night to perch on large rocks in mid-stream. Arboreal frogs vary in their selection of perches; the Cinnamon Tree Frog (*Nyctixalus pictus*) and the Frilled Tree Frog (*Rhacophorus appendiculatus*) sit on the leaves of shrubs and young trees whereas others, particularly larger species such as File-eared Tree Frog (*Polypedates otilophus*) and the Brown Tree Toad (*Pedostibes hosii*) perch on twigs, branches or even trunks of small trees. One of the persistent mysteries of tree frogs concerns the heights at which they feed and rest. A human observer on the ground can spot frogs only to a certain height, perhaps up to eight metres. Seeing a frog at a distance further than that, especially with one's line of sight hindered by branches and leaves is extremely difficult. Nevertheless, we know frogs do live higher up because we have heard them calling from the canopy.

The microhabitats of tadpoles, though not as varied as those of adult frogs, still cover a broad range of conditions. Despite the necessity for living in water, tadpoles possess a tremendous number of specializations within particular types of aquatic habitats. Even among species that live in a single stream there can be major differences. For example, there are tadpoles found only in the swift or turbulent portions of rocky streams (Fig. 11), such as frogs of the genus *Meristogenys*, which cling to rocks in extremely strong currents by means of an abdominal sucker. These same stretches of water are also used by tadpoles of the Spiny Slender Toad (*Ansonia spinulifer*), which differs by using its expanded lips as a clinging device, an adaptation seen in a number of Bornean freshwater fishes. Other kinds of tadpoles may be present in the rapids, but these wriggle down into the crevices between rocks and gravel at the bottom, including larvae of the slender litter frogs (*Leptolalax* spp.) and the Short-nosed Tree Frog (*Rhacophorus gauni*).

Fig. 11. Rapids on rocky forest stream.

Accumulations of dead leaves may form in streams where the topography creates eddies, pockets of little or no current at the side of a rapid. These leaf drifts form the principal microhabitat of other kinds of tadpoles, including those of the Giant River Frog (*Rana leporina*), the Spotted Stream Frog (*Rana picturata),* the Brown Slender Toad (*Ansonia leptopus*) and the Brown Tree Toad (*Pedostibes hosei*). These four species are sometimes found in quiet, sheltered side pools cut off from the main current flow by a gravel bar, or rocks. These placid pools with their silt-laden bottoms are also the main habitat of another set of tadpole species, including those of the White-lipped Frog (*Rana chalconota*), the Crested Toad ((*Bufo divergens*) and the Harlequin Tree Frog (*Rhacophorus pardalis*).

Some stream tadpoles, such as those of the large-eyed litter frogs (*Leptobrachium* spp.) seem to thrive in a variety of microhabitats no matter what the current strength or bottom type. Somehow these large, fat tadpoles can maintain themselves without "streamlining" or special clinging adaptations even in stretches of moderately strong current.

Silty pools on the forest floor are the main type of environment for tadpoles of several tree frogs and those of several inconspicuous dwarf species such as the Bornean Narrow-mouthed Frog (*Microhyla borneensis*). Usually a rhino or pig wallow (Fig. 8), or isolated forest rain pool will hold several kinds of tadpoles: a tree frog tadpole and one or two terrestrial dwarf species. In these small communities, the two or three types of tadpoles differ greatly in size and mode of feeding. The tree frog tadpoles (*Rhacophorus nigropalmatus* or *Rhacophorus reinwardtii*, for example) are at least twice as long as the others, and feed by "rooting" or "grubbing" in the decaying organic matter at the bottom. The smaller tadpoles (*Microhyla borneensis*) hover in mid-water and filter out food particles as they pump water through the mouth cavity and over the gills.

Tiny pools of water, sometimes no more than 1 cm deep and 10 cm across, which collect on the surface of rotten logs or even on large, dead leaves can provide suitable habitats for tadpoles of the Rufous-sided Sticky Frog (*Kalophrynus pleurostigma*) or of one of the small forest toads of the genus *Pelophryne*. Tadpoles of these species do not feed, but instead complete their development by absorbing the large amount of yolk within relatively large eggs. Development to metamorphosis takes place in 7–10 days, and when the young froglets hop away from their birth pool, they are hardly as large as a medium-sized ant.

Pockets of water above the ground in tree holes or buttress troughs are the microhabitats of another group of tree frogs. These elevated microhabitats illustrate one of the major differences between tadpoles and frogs. Obviously, tadpoles cannot "find" a place to live in the usual sense nor can they migrate from one habitat to another. They develop wherever the eggs are laid. Thus, if eggs are placed in tree holes, that is where the tadpoles must live or die. Nevertheless, a situation could arise within a stream that is prone to flooding, in which there could be some involuntary movement between habitats. Although little is known for certain, given the often powerful but short-lived nature of floods in Borneo's hill streams, tadpoles washed out of a sheltered pool probably are not likely to survive the turbulent journey to a new one.

One of the strangest and most intriguing of the frog life cycles in Borneo is that of the "guardian frogs" (*Rana finchi* and *Rana palavanensis*). Both of these species lay eggs on the forest floor, which are initially guarded by the male (Fig. 12). As the tadpoles hatch, they somehow

Fig. 12. *Rana finchi* male guarding eggs.

attach to his back (Fig. 13) and are carried around for an unknown period of time, perhaps several days, until the parent frog encounters a suitable pool. The male moves into the water and larvae swim away and complete their development in the pool. The purpose of this odd behaviour must certainly be protection for the larvae, but the conditions that led to its evolution are not yet understood.

Like other frogs of Southeast Asia, the frogs of Borneo are entirely carnivorous, taking only animals as food. Overall, they prey primarily on insects and related invertebrates such as spiders. Most frogs eat a wide variety of prey within certain size limits, but some have rather specialised diets. The Rufous-Sided Sticky Frog (*Kalophrynus pleurostigma*) feeds mostly on ants and termites, so of course most of its prey are small. These modest-sized frogs can eat from 50–150 ants or termites at a single sitting. The frog will often park itself at the entrance to an ant or termite nest, or by a "parade" of these food items, and pack its tummy at a leisurely pace. The Crested Toad (*Bufo divergens*) while feeding on a wide assortment of insects, also leans toward a diet rich in ants and termites. Stomachs of this species when examined contained on average about 64% ants and 31% termites, and an average of 43 prey

36

items per stomach. The Giant River Toad (*Bufo juxtasper*) follows a similar pattern despite its large size. The main difference between the two toads lies in the prey size, with the river toad eating larger prey (average 7.4 mm) and the crested toad, smaller (average 4.0 mm). It is no mystery why ants and termites form a major diet component for some of these forest frogs, since these invertebrates form the largest element of animal biomass in Southeast Asian tropical forests.

R.B. Stuebing

Fig. 13. *Rana finchi* male carrying tadpoles.

The majority of Bornean frogs are, however, dietary generalists, even though ants still remain an important food type for many of them. The smooth guardian frog, a small (average 20–30 mm) species, consumes spiders, beetles, katydids and other orthopterans but ants are nevertheless more than 50% of its prey. As a rule, the generalists tend to eat larger prey and to ingest fewer prey per meal. For example, five stomachs of the Abbott's Litter Frog (*Leptobrachium abbotti*) contained crickets, spiders and a cockroach, all with an average length of 17.5 mm; the average number was only 1.5 prey items. The Common Horned Frog (*Megophrys nasuta*) with its impressively wide mouth eats even larger prey (average 32 mm), and willing to tackle and swallow 4 cm snails and 10 cm scorpions. The largest prey of all are taken by the Giant River

Frog (*Rana leporina*), the Mud Frog (*Rana malesiana*) and the Greater Swamp Frog (*Rana ingeri*), some of Borneo's largest species. These eat frogs, snakes, crabs, forest millipedes, scorpions; almost any small animal passing too close to one of these adult frogs is likely to disappear in a single gulp.

The individual breeding and feeding habits of frogs in Borneo has led to interesting patterns of distribution among them. For example, as in some other vertebrate groups, distinct communities of frogs exist at various altitudes, undoubtedly caused by radically different habitats in different topography and at different altitudes. Recognisable frog communities occur in mangrove where, because most frogs cannot tolerate even mild salinity, only the Mangrove or Crab-Eating Frog (*Rana cancrivora*) and

occasionally the Taiwanese Frog (*Rana rugulosa*) can be found. Other distinct communities can be seen in peat swamp (Fig. 13), with numerous Swamp Frogs (*Rana malesiana* and *Rana paramacrodon*), rufous Toads (*Bufo quadriporcatus*) and rough-sided frogs (*Rana glandulosa*); a much richer community can, of course be found in the hilly lowlands (Fig. 7), with numerous members of the genera *Meristogenys*, *Rana*, *Kalophrynus*, *Ansonia*, *Rhacophorus* and others. Interestingly, this community is again different above about 1,200 metres in elevation. Perhaps because of the steep topography the meandering streams with their numerous microhabitats are increasingly rare. Stronger currents caused by more extreme gradients lead also to fewer opportunities for organic material to collect, and to more "catastrophic" stream flows, washing out detritus (as well as any resident tadpoles!). Thus, at higher altitudes there is a significant absence of frogs from certain families or genera. Above 3000 metres there are no megophryids, few bufonids and few microhylids. The most abundant species are tree or bush frogs of the genera *Rhacophorus* and *Philautus.* The reasons for this appear to be directly related to breeding: the frogs that remain are those which do not depend on streams to breed. Some, such as the most common genus, *Philautus,* show tendencies towards direct development of the tadpoles within the egg, eliminating the free-swimming tadpole stage entirely. There are also interesting opportunists, such as the tiny (average length about 15 mm) Black Toad *Pelophryne misera*, which deposits its eggs in the water-filled reservoirs of pitcher plants. Thus, there is here a hint that frog communities may be crafted not so much by what the adults can do, but under what conditions their tadpoles can survive.

All of this ecological information can actually be summarized rather simply: frogs have succeeded in exploiting almost every imaginable nook and cranny of Borneo's forests, and to use in one way or another essentially all the insects or other invertebrates found there. Tadpoles expand further the range of environments and food resources used by the adult frogs. Furthermore, the species making up this rich fauna divide and share resources of space and food, forming a critical part of the complex structure of the tropical rain forest.

Fig. 14 (opposite). Stream in peat swamp.

CHAPTER 5

CONSERVATION

D uring the early 1990s, the attention of biologists was suddenly drawn towards the decline in numbers or even the disappearance, either gradual or abrupt, of various species of frogs in locations in North and Central America, Europe and Australia. No one was surprised that one or several species disappeared when the environment was drastically disturbed, for example by the clearing forest or the conversion of a native grassland to a wheat field. But what concerned biologists was the declines that took place in protected, undisturbed environments. Populations in a variety of habitat types, from mountain ponds to coastal streams, declined or disappeared. A number of causes have been suggested, including pollution (such as pesticides, herbicides, fertilizers, or acid rain), genetic damage caused by increased exposure to ultraviolet light (implicating the loss of the earth's ozone layer) and pathogens (such as lethal viruses). So far, however, no single factor linking all these apparent declines has been identified.

In Borneo, based on our work and that of our colleagues over the last 40 years, there is no evidence of any decline in Bornean frogs in undisturbed forests. Fluctuations in populations, both up and down and sometimes dramatic, have been observed, but no long-term trends are apparent. Though the hunting of frogs for food has occasionally been blamed for a loss of these amphibians from their habitats (as in the ricefields of Bangladesh in the late 1980s), human consumption of frogs is rarely a problem in most cases, compared at least to human modification of natural habitats. The only native species (that is, those living in undisturbed forest habitats) that are probably affected by hunting are the large, long-lived, slow growing species, such as, the Giant River Frog (*Rana leporina*) and its relatives.

Less than ten per cent of the Bornean amphibian fauna, and not a single uniquely Bornean species, can thrive in habitats greatly modified by people. Though some studies show that selective logging is one of the human activities least damaging to anuran communities, most of the forest exploitation currently practiced does result in noticeable "community shifts", in which certain species increase and others become much more difficult to find. For example, the silted streams of logged areas in Sarawak show an increase in the giant river frog (*Rana leporina*), while some species of Torrent Frogs (*Meristogenys* spp.) become scarce. The explanation lies in the reproductive habits of these species. The giant river frog is not sensitive to turbidity and selects shallow sand bars to lay its eggs, while its tadpoles feed on suspended organic debris such as dead leaves. Torrent frogs, on the other hand, need clear water for successful breeding, and their tadpoles feed on the thin film of microscopic organisms growing on the clean surface of rocks and boulders. In logged areas, rocks in streams become coated with a thin layer of silt, and the food supply of these tadpoles is destroyed. Nevertheless, research has also revealed that many species, even sensitive ones, can return if the surrounding forest is allowed to remain undisturbed for five to ten years.

Agriculture creates special problems for the native frog fauna. Not only does agriculture, like complete timber extraction, remove the natural habitat and increase the silt load in streams; it also introduces many chemicals, pesticides, herbicides, fertilizers, etc., that affect the fauna adversely. With the increase the size of the human population, it is inevitable that more land in Borneo will be converted to agriculture, which will lead to increased siltation, chemical pollution, and increased runoof and flooding after heavy rains.

If we want to preserve Borneo's frog fauna, which is among the richest anywhere in the world, it will be necessary to preserve a variety of natural, original habitats at a variety of places in Borneo. That is, of course, the same recipe for preserving most of Borneo's plant and animal species.

CHAPTER 6

FAMILY BOMBINATORIDAE

T his family occurs in eastern Asia and in Central Europe. The genus to which the Bornean species belongs is found only in Borneo and the Palawan group (Philippine Islands). This is one of the oldest groups of frogs and *Barbourula* is unusual because it seems to lead an entirely aquatic existence. (See also Chapter 4).

Barbourula kalimantanensis Iskandar
Flat-Headed Frog (Fig. 15)

Description: A medium-sized frog with a flattened head and broad, rounded snout. This frog has a number of distinctive features. The fingers and toes are fully webbed to the tips, and the tips of both fingers and toes are slightly swollen. A distinct flap of skin runs along the outer finger. The third and fourth toes are about the same length as are the second and third fingers; the effect is to make both hand and foot look like rounded paddles. There is a small conical projection of skin just below the front third of the eye. The eardrum is missing. The back is rough, with many small, spiny or rounded skin projections, and there are folds of skin along the sides of the body and along the thigh and lower leg. The entire frog is dark brown or black, with lighter mottling on the underside.
Male: 68 mm.
Female: 77 mm.

Tadpole: Unknown.

Habits and habitat: Only two specimens of this odd species have ever been found, both caught when boulders were overturned in shallow, swift water and both caught in the same area. The species is clearly fully aquatic, but nothing else is known of its habits.

43

Distribution: Known only from the middle of the Kapuas River basin in western Kalimantan.

Fig. 15. *Barbourula kalimantanensis* Iskandar.

CHAPTER 7

FAMILY MEGOPHRYIDAE

The Bornean species used to be classified as members of the Family Pelobatidae and were so listed in *Frogs of Sabah*.

Genus *Leptobrachella*
Dwarf Litter Frogs

The genus *Leptobrachella* includes the smallest adult frogs in the family Megophryidae, and is known only from Borneo and the Bungaran (sometimes called Natunas) Islands. There are six species in Borneo and three, *Leptobrachella mjöbergi* (Sarawak), *L. baluensis* (Sabah), and *L. parva* (Sabah), are relatively common. None have been reported yet from Brunei or Kalimantan, but this absence merely reflects the lack of field exploration in those areas.

Adults and juveniles wander over the forest floor leaf litter, where they forage for very small insects and other invertebrates. Adults are most commonly seen along the banks of clear, rocky streams about 1–2 metres wide, where they congregate to breed. Males call while sitting on dead leaves on the bank or perched on leaves of herbs 10–20 cm above the ground. For their size *Leptobrachella* species are some of the loudest frogs in Borneo. They have an extremely intense, high-pitched, metallic trill. Large numbers of breeding males along streams can drown out even some of the night insects of the forest. Tadpoles of Dwarf Litter Frogs live in crevices between gravel and small rocks on the bed of riffles, sharing this environment with tadpoles of the Slender Litter Frogs. These frogs have been found from 150 to 2200 metres above sea level, with two species, *L. baluensis* and *L. brevicrus* restricted to elevations above 900 metres.

Description—adults: All species are tiny (less than 25 mm), with the head slightly narrower than the body. The most unusual feature of these little frogs is the pointed, almost triangular expansions at the tips of the fingers. The eardrum is visible, and the skin is smooth. All species except *L. palmata* lack webbing on the feet. The general colouration is dark brown or black with dark markings on the back. Usually there are small black spots on the sides. Colouration of the belly varies among the species.
Males: 15–19 mm
Females: 18–22 mm

Tadpoles: Larvae are grayish and extremely elongated like the tadpoles of Slender Litter Frogs. Although tadpoles of both groups have heavy black beaks, those of the Dwarf Litter Frogs lack the rows of fine, tiny teeth present on the lips of tadpoles of the Slender Litter Frogs. When ready to metamorphose, *Leptobrachella* tadpoles measure 40–47 mm.

Leptobrachella baluensis Smith
Kinabalu Dwarf Litter Frog

Description: A small, slender species lacking webbing on the foot. The skin is smooth on the back; the sides have a few light-coloured glands. The colour is brown or black, with several black spots on the back and a sharply defined, black streak over the eardrum. The sides have 1–4 large black spots. The belly is dark gray with small light spots.
Males: 15–19 mm.
Females: 18–21 mm.

Tadpoles: See description under genus.

Habits and habitat: This species has been found only in submontane and montane forests from 900 to 2200 metres above sea level. See also under genus.

Call: See under genus.

Distribution: This species has been found only in the mountains of western Sabah and northern Sarawak.

Leptobrachella mjöbergi Smith
Mjöberg's Dwarf Litter Frog (Fig. 16)

Description: A small, slender species lacking webbing on the foot. The skin is smooth on the back, while the sides have elongate glands forming a low, narrow, broken ridge. The colour is brown or black, with several black spots on the back. There is no black streak over the eardrum. The chest is flecked with brown or has a brown network; the rest of the belly is usually unmarked.
Males: 17–20 mm.
Females: 18–21 mm.

Tadpoles: See description under genus.

Habits and habitat: This species lives in hilly lowland forests from 150 to 500 metres above sea level and breeds along small, clear, rocky streams. See also under genus.

Distribution: So far known only from Sarawak, though it is to be expected in Kalimantan.

R.B. Stuebing

Fig. 16. *Leptobrachella mjöbergi* Smith.

Leptobrachella palmata Inger & Stuebing
Webfooted Dwarf Litter Frog

Description: This is the smallest species in the genus, and the only one with well-developed webbing on the foot. The back and belly are smooth, while the sides have scattered round glands. The upper surfaces are medium brown, without markings except for dark crossbars on the limbs. The sides have a dark metwork enclosing the white glands. The middle of the belly is light, without markings.
Males: 14–17 mm.
Females: Unknown.

Tadpole: Unknown.

Habits and habitat: The only known specimens were found along a stream bank in hilly forest at 350 metres above sea level.

Distribution: Known only from a single site in the interior of Sabah.

Leptobrachella parva Dring
Rough-Sided Dwarf Litter Frog

Description: A small species lacking webbing. The sides have small, rounded, scattered glands (lumps), while the back is smooth. The general colouration is similar to *L. baluensis*, but the sides lack large black spots, though there may be small black dots. Some individuals have a dark area over the eardrum, but it is not sharply defined like the streak in *L. baluensis*. The belly is dark.
Males: 15–19 mm.
Females: 19 mm.

Tadpole: See under genus.

Habits and habitat: Like others in the genus, this species lives in hillly forests where clear, gravel or rock-bottomed streams exist. Its known elevational range is 150 to 750 metres above sea level.

Distribution: All of Sabah and northern part of Sarawak.

Leptobrachella serasanae Dring
Striped Dwarf Litter Frog

Description: Toes with little or no webbing. The sides have a few small, rounded glands. *Leptobrachella serasanae* is the only species in the genus having a continuous black streak from the eye to the groin.
Males: 17–19 mm.
Females: 20 mm.

Tadpole: Unknown.

Habits and habitat: Adults have been found on the banks of small streams and amidst the leaf litter in hilly, lowland forest.

Distribution: In Borneo, known so far only from southeastern Sarawak. This species also occurs on Pulo Serasan, in the Bungaran Islands, only 80 km off the coast of Borneo.

Genus *Leptobrachium*
Large-eyed Litter Frogs

Previously, the most widely distributed species of *Leptobrachium* in Borneo was referred to as *Leptobrachium montanum* Fischer. Field work over the last ten years, however, has revealed consistent differences between lowland and highland (above approx. 1000 metres) forms of "*L. montanum*." Females of the high elevations are smaller, and all adults invariably show a chalky white eye-ring and have plain, grayish bellies; lowland forms have larger females, and all adults have a bold pattern of black and white on the underside and no discernible eye ring. A small percentage of Sarawak frogs from the lowlands have no belly pattern. These and other differences between the lowland and highland forms has required revision of the species names. Based on type specimens collected more than half a century ago, the names assigned to these species are *Leptobrachium abbottii* for the lowland form and *Leptobrachium montanum* for the high elevation species. Two other species, *L. hendricksoni* and *L. nigrops*, are known only from coastal areas of Sarawak.

Adults and juveniles live in the forest floor leaf litter, where they feed on rather large insects. The frogs sit peculiarly erect, but bow low into a crouch when disturbed by a heavy foot step or a flashlight. With their slender, short hind limbs, these frogs are capable only of short hops. Adults migrate to small or medium-sized streams to breed and lay their eggs in quiet pools. The tadpoles remain in side pools or open pools of streams, hiding under rocks during the day. Tadpoles feed on bits of dead vegetation, which they snip into bits with their large, heavy beaks.

Description—adult: All species are of moderate size, with females larger than males. All are stocky frogs with slender, short hind limbs and a head that is slightly wider than the body. The eardrum is visible. The tips of the fingers and toes are rounded, except for *L. nigrops*, which has distinctly curved and pointed fingers. The skin is smooth, with a curved ridge over the eardrum. All species have dark brown to black colouration, usually with a faint, complex darker pattern on the top of the head and back.
Males: 35–75 mm.
Females: 37–95 mm.

Tadpoles: The tadpoles of all species are large, heavy-bodied and oval in body shape. The tail is long, shaped like a narrow leaf, and tapers gradually to a blunt tip. The tadpoles become heavily spotted with black as they grow. The actual pattern of spotting varies with the species. Just before metamorphosis the tadpoles reach 70–90 mm in total length.

Leptobrachium abbotti Cochran
Lowland Litter Frog (Fig. 17)

Description: A stocky, broad-headed frog with bulging eyes. The legs are short and slender and seem almost too small for a frog of this size. The toes have almost no webbing. The skin is smooth. The head, back, and sides are dark brown to black, with a faint dark pattern usually evident only on the top of the head. The belly is heavily marked with a bold black and white mottling. Some individual frogs from Sarawak may have a white or gray unmarked belly.
Males: 43–75 mm.
Females: 60–95 mm.

Fig. 17. *Leptobrachium abbotti* Cochran.

Tadpoles: The tadpoles are large, reaching 75–90 mm by the time they are ready to metamorphose. At hatching they are pale brown to straw-coloured, but gradually darken into medium brown and develop large black spots on the body and tail. The first spots to appear are those at the end of the body or base of the tail.

Habits and habitat: Juveniles and adults live within the dead leaves and litter on the floor of primary and old secondary growth forests below 1000 metres above sea level. The species has not been found in swampy forest. The food consists of large insects and other invertebrates. Adults move to small or medium-sized streams to breed and lay their eggs in quiet pools. The males do not form calling aggregations, and it is unusual to see more than one or two males on a given night.

The tadpoles hide under rocks at the bottom of pools in the centre or at the sides of streams. They feed on dead and decaying vegetation falling into the stream, and can snip off large bits with their heavy beaks.

Call: A single, resonant, squawking note.

Distribution: Known from all parts of Borneo below 1000 metres above sea level.

51

Leptobrachium hendricksoni Taylor
Spotted Litter Frog (Fig. 18)

Description: Like the Lowland Litter Frog, with wide head, large eye, short legs, and almost no webbing. The species is more brownish or reddish than the Lowland Litter Frog but also lacks a conspicuous dark belly pattern. The underside is white or cream-coloured with many small black dots.
Males: 45–50 mm.
Females: 63 mm.

Tadpoles: Large and heavy as in the Lowland Litter Frog. Body and tail pale brown, with many small black dots.

Habits and habitat: So far this species has only been found in flat, swampy forests. Tadpoles live in quiet pools of slow flowing streams.

Call: Unknown.

R.B. Stuebing

Fig. 18. *Leptobrachium hendricksoni* Taylor.

Distribution: Known only from areas near the coast of Sarawak. Although not yet reported from Kalimantan, it probably occurs in the swampy, lowlands that cross the southern parts of that state. It may also occur in the peaty areas near the southwestern coast of Sabah and in Brunei. this species also occurs in Peninsular Malaysia.

Leptobrachium montanum (Fischer)
Montane Litter Frog (Fig. 19)

Description: Like the Lowland Litter Frog in head width and body shape, with the same under-sized hind limbs. The skin is smooth. Colouration is like the Lowland Litter Frog except usually lighter and more brown than black. The dark pattern on the back and head is more conspicuous than in the lowland form. A narrow, bluish white ring curves around the eyeball and is normally visible at the edge of the eyelid. The belly is always a dirty gray without markings.

Males: 46–63 mm.

Females: 50–65 mm.

R.B. Stuebing

Fig. 19. *Leptobrachium montanum* (Fischer).

53

Tadpoles: Like those of the lowland form.

Habits and habitat: This species lives in submontane and montane forests higher than 900 metres above sea level. The highest record we know of is 1680 metres. Other habits as in lowland form.

Call: A single resonant, squawking note.

Distribution: Reported from northern, northwestern, and southwestern Borneo. Presumably, occurs throughout Borneo above 900 metres.

Leptobrachium nigrops Berry & Hendrickson
Black-eyed Litter Frog (Fig. 20)

Description: Smaller and with narrower head than other species, but still a stocky frog with short hind legs. As in the other species of this genus, the toes are almost without webbing. The fingers have a distinct, sharp curve near the tips, which are pointed. The sharp, bony finger tips can actually hurt a person grasping one of these frogs. Skin smooth or with low ridges. The colour is gray to brown, with a conspicuous pattern of black, oval spots on upper surfaces. The eye is decidedly black.
Males: 35–40 mm.
Females: 37–50 mm.

Fig. 20. *Leptobrachium nigrops* Berry & Hendrickson.

Tadpoles: Shaped like those of other *Leptobrachium*. Distinguished by a golden stripe down the centre of the back. Maximum size 75 mm.

Habits and habitat: This species has been found in both flat and hilly forests and in swampy terrain. Tadpoles live in very slowly moving water.

Call: Unknown.

Distribution: In Borneo, it has been reported only from coastal areas of Sarawak. The species also occurs in Peninsular Malaysia.

Genus *Leptolalax*
Slender Litter Frogs

At least five species of this genus occur in Borneo. All have the same general appearance and the same general habits. These are frogs of the forest floor, though occasionally an individual will perch on an herb or a low branch of a shrub. They feed on small insects and other invertebrates; the prey is rarely move than 10 mm. Adults move to small or medium-sized, clear streams to breed. There may be many adults at a stream on a particular night, but they do not clump together. The calls consist of a series of pulsating, high-pitched notes, varying slightly in the number of notes per call and in pitch (according to Prof. M. Matsui). Although eggs have not been found, we presume that they are laid under rocks. The tadpoles wriggle into the crevices between rocks on the bottom of riffles and are remarkably elongate and slender.

Description—adults: Slender frogs with the head not much wider than the body. The eye is very large, its diameter usually longer than the snout. The eardrum is visible. The limbs are slender and the hind limb is very long. Fingers and toes have rounded tips and the toes are almost without webbing. The skin of the back and sides is usually rough with small rounded or elongate lumps and ridges. The belly is smooth. The colour is gray to dark brown, usually with a pattern of black spots on the back and sides.
Males: 26–39 mm.
Females: 21–48 mm.

Tadpoles: Tadpoles are long and slender and have a heavily muscled tail with very low fins. The eyes are small. The entire tadpole is dark gray without markings. Although they have heavy, black beaks like tadpoles of *Leptobrachium*, their rows of teeth are much reduced. Just before metamorphosis the tadpoles are 50–55 mm long.

Leptolalax dringi Dubois
Dring's Slender Litter Frog (Fig. 21)

Description: A slender, large-eyed frog, with moderately long, slender hind limbs. Toes lack webbing. These frogs have small, round lumps on the back and sides, and especially on the top of the snout. The back and top of head are grayish brown, often with tinges of reddish brown. There are usually black markings on the back and head, but often these are obscured by the dark background, particularly on the head. The chest and belly have small black spots. The elbow may be lighter, but is not sharply set off from the colour of the rest of the fore limb.
Males: 30–35 mm.
Females: 37–48 mm.

Tadpole: See under genus.

Habits and habitat: This species lives in primary and old secondary forests in hilly to mountainous country from 200 to 1800 metres above sea level.

Distribution: *Leptolalax dringi* has been reported from the northern part of Sarawak and from the whole of Sabah.

Leptolalax gracilis (Günther)
Sarawak Slender Litter Frog (Fig. 22)

Description: Shape similar to the preceding species. Webbing only at base of toes. Skin rough above and on sides, with small, round lumps and short, low ridges.

C.L. Chan

Fig. 21 (above). *Leptolalax dringi* Dubois. **Fig. 22** (below). *Leptolalax gracilis* (Günther).

R.B. Stuebing

The frogs are dark brown above and on sides, with obscure dark spots on back and head. The sides have light and dark spots with light centres. The chest and belly are heavily marked with dark brown or black spots. The fore limb has a light cream area at the elbow, sharply contrasting with the dark upper and lower arm.

Males: 31–39 mm.

Females: 40–48 mm.

Tadpole: See under genus.

Habits and habitat: This species lives in primary and old secondary growth forests in hilly country. Breeding takes place at small to large streams with clear water and sandy to rocky bottoms.

Distribution: This species has been found throughout Sarawak below 500 metres.

R.B. Stuebing

Fig. 23. *Leptolalax hamidi* Matsui.

Leptolalax hamidi Matsui
White-Bellied Slender Litter Frog (Fig. 23)

Description: Very similar to *L. pictus*. The toes are webbed at the base. The skin is smooth. The colouration is very similar to *L. pictus*, with light-bordered black markings on the medium brown back and head. The belly is white or cream-coloured without spots. The fore limb does not have a sharply defined light area at the elbow.
Males: 29–31 mm.
Females: 37–41 mm.

Tadpole: Unknown.

Habits and habitat: This species lives in hilly primary and old secondary forest from 100 to 250 metres above sea level.

Distribution: This species has been collected in the southern half of Sarawak and in central Kalimantan.

Leptolalax maura Inger, Maklarin, Alim & Yambun
Montane Slender Litter Frog

Description: This is a relatively stocky, small frog. The toes are webbed only at the base. The back has many low, rounded lumps and slightly larger warts on the sides. The colour is very dark brown or black; there is no visible pattern on the back. This is the only species in the genus that is uniformly dark brown on the underside of the head and hind limbs. The fore limb does not have contrasting light and dark colouration.
Male: 26 mm.
Female: 32 mm.

Tadpole: Unknown.

Habits and habitat: This species has only been collected once, making it difficult to draw conclusions about habits. The only collecting site was in montane forest at 1850 m on Mount Kinabalu.

Distribution: Known only from Mount Kinabalu in Sabah.

Leptolalax pictus Malkmus
Painted Slender Litter Frog (Fig. 24)

Description: Similar in shape to *L. gracilis*. The toes are webbed at the base. Skin smooth, at most a few lumps on the sides. The colour is light to medium brown, with conspicuous, light-edged, dark markings on back and head. The side of the head has sharply defined blackish brown spots. The belly is white without spots. The fore limb lacks contrasting light and dark colouration.
Males: 31–36 mm.
Females: 39–47 mm.

Tadpole: Unknown.

Habits and habitat: This species, like the others, lives in primary and old secondary growth forest. It does not occur at low elevations, having been found from 500 to 1540 metres.

Distribution: Western parts of Sabah.

R.F. Inger

Fig. 24. *Leptolalax pictus* Malkmus.

60

Genus *Megophrys*
Horned Frogs

Two features of the Bornean species of Horned Frogs stand out: large, wide heads and projections of skin from their eyelids, the so-called "horns." The species are not identical in the form taken by these "horns," but they all have them. Their large heads and very wide mouths suggest an ability to take in relatively large prey—which is exactly what they do. Snails with shells 50 mm wide are no problem for their enormous mouths. Large prey items, mostly insects but also centipedes and scorpions, are the rule for these species.

The slender legs are incapable of launching these heavy-bodied terrestrial frogs away from a potential enemy; the Horned Frogs merely hop short distances. Since flight is out of the question, they rely on camouflage. All have the general brown or reddish brown colour of the dead leaves amidst which they spend their lives. Several species have long, low ridges on the back, which resemble the veins on dead leaves, while the sharp "horns" and snout of *Megophrys nasuta* resemble the curled, pointed leaf tips. *Megophrys edwardinae* has odd projections from the skin of the head and back, breaking up the outline of the body.

Juveniles and adults live on the forest floor in primary and old secondary growth forests from 60 to 1900 metres above sea level. During the day, they retreat beneath dead leaves (juveniles) or dead logs or large rocks (adults). Adults move to the banks of small to medium-sized streams to breed. These migrations must be slow processes, considering how far from streams the adults roam and the short distance they cover in the average hop. The loud honk of *Megophrys nasuta* in advance of heavy rain is one of the characteristic sounds of the lowland rain forest in late afternoon or evening. Eggs are laid in pools at the edge of streams and the tadpoles live in riffles or quiet side pools. These tadpoles have a remarkable way of feeding: they hang from the surface with their funnel-mouths (see below) spread and filter out small bits of organic matter caught in the surface film.

Description—adults: *Megophrys* are medium-sized to large frogs, with very large, wide heads and slender, relatively short hind limbs. The toes are not webbed. In all but one Bornean species (*M. dringi*), the head width almost equals half the combined head-plus-body length. The diameter of the eye is about equal to the length of the snout. The upper eyelid has a projection of skin in some form, varying among the species. Thickened skin partially obscures the eardrum in several species. Most species have thin, narrow ridges of skin at least on the front part of the back. All species have a strong, curved ridge or fold of skin from the eye, curving over the eardrum and ending at the arm pit.

Males: 39–104 mm.

Females: 55–125 mm.

Tadpoles: The tadpoles are slender and dark with blackish markings on the tail. Their most remarkable feature is the mouth. In all Bornean tadpoles but those of *Megophrys*, the mouth points downward and is at the bottom of the snout. In tadpoles of *Megophrys*, the lips are widened and turned upward, so that the mouth forms a funnel at the same level as the top of the head. Total length at metamorphosis is 40–45 mm.

Call: The voice of only one species, *M. nasuta*, is known and consists of a single, loud honk. This sharp, multi-toned note is emitted at intervals.

Megophrys baluensis (Boulenger)
Kinabalu Horned Frog (Fig. 25)

Description: A stocky medium-sized to large frog, with short, slender hind limbs. The head width is almost equal to half the head-plus-body length. The eardrum is visible. A short, narrow, triangular "horn" projects from the upper eyelid, which also has several shorter, vertical projections. The back has one long, interrupted, thin ridge of skin on each side and a few scattered short ridges and round lumps. The upper surfaces are brown or reddish brown, usually with a dark triangular mark between the eyes. The side of the head is dark brown, sometimes with a narrow yellow stripe at the edge of the snout.

Males: 41–45 mm.

Females: 55–70 mm.

Fig. 25 (opposite). *Megophrys baluensis* (Boulenger).

Tadpole: See under genus.

Habits and habitat: This species lives in montane forests from 1200 to 1900 metres. See also under genus.

Distribution: Known from mountains of western Sabah and northern Sarawak.

R.B. Stuebing

Megophrys dringi Inger, Stuebing & Tan
Dring's Horned Frog

Description: A stocky frog, with slender hind limbs. The width of the head is about one-third the length of head-plus-body. The eardrum is partly hidden by skin. The upper eyelid has a narrow, short, projecting "horn." A short, weak fold of skin runs back from the eye part way down the body, and somtimes a pair of weak ridges forms a V on the front of the torso. Colour grayish or reddish brown, sometimes with a dark triangular mark between the eyes.
Males: 43–47 mm.
Females: 55 mm.

Tadpole: Unknown.

Habits and habitat: Julian Dring, the discoverer of this species, found adults at the edges of a steep, swift stream in montane forest at 1800 metres.

Distribution: Known so far only from Mount Mulu, Sarawak.

Megophrys edwardinae Inger
Rough Horned Frog (Fig. 26)

Description: A stocky, medium-sized frog, with slender legs. The width of the head equals half the head-plus-body length. The eardrum is mostly hidden by skin. The "horn" is a drawn-out, slender, triangular projection from the eyelid. The head and body are covered with many irregular, round or a bit elongated, ridges or projections of skin, including one pointed projection at the corners of the mouth and several vertical ones on the eyelid.

The general colour is clay brown, with black bars on the side of the head and across the limbs. A large dark marking usually covers much of the back.
Males: 39–42 mm.
Females: 70–82 mm.

Tadpole: See under genus.

Habits and habitat: This species lives in hilly or steep lowland rain forest. Juveniles and adults feed on the forest floor and hide under dead leaves and logs during the day. Adults move to small, clear, rocky streams to breed.

Distribution: Sarawak and western Sabah, between 200 and 600 metres above sea level.

Fig. 26. *Megophrys edwardinae* Inger.

Megophrys nasuta (Schlegel)
Bornean Horned Frog (Fig. 27)

Description: A very stocky, medium-sized to large frog, with short, slender legs. The width of the head is half the head-plus-body length. The "horn" is a very wide, pointed, triangular projection from the edge of the eyelid. Most individuals of this species also have a similar pointed projection from the tip of the snout. The back has two pairs of long, narrow folds of skin. The colour is light clay to reddish brown, sometimes with one or two dark spots on the back. Usually there is a wide, dark bar on the side of the head below the eye.

Males: 70–105 mm.

Females: 90–125 mm.

Tadpole: See under genus.

Habits and habitat: This species appears to be the most widely distributed and common one in the genus. It lives in flat to steep rain forests, from near sea level to about 1600 metres. Adults breed at streams having weak to moderate currents. Tadpoles live in riffles, and are frequently found hiding where root mats of bank vegetation trail in the water. See also under genus.

Distribution: Found throughout Borneo. It also occurs in Sumatra and Peninsular Malaysia.

R.B. Stuebing

Fig. 27. *Megophrys nasuta* (Schlegel).

CHAPTER 8

FAMILY BUFONIDAE (TRUE TOADS)

This family has a world-wide distribution, but Borneo and Southeast Asia have a distinctive set of genera and species.

Genus *Ansonia*
Slender Toads

These relatively small, slender toads have the dry, rough skin of typical toads, but lack the large parotoid gland behind the eye and above the ear drum characteristic of most toads. Although the genus occurs in the Philippine Islands and Peninsular Malaysia, Borneo is where most species (12) occur.

The species of *Ansonia* are restricted to primary and old secondary forests, including selectively logged forests, in hilly to mountainous country from the lowlands to 3000 metres above sea level. Adults live on the forest floor but are occasionally seen on leaves of herbaceous plants. Ants and other small insects make up the diets of the four species that have been studied; probably all the species have similar diets. Adults move to clear, rocky streams to breed, where they perch on rocks, small shrubs, or herbs near rapids. Tadpoles, with the exception of *A. leptopus*, live in swift currents attached to rocks, situations requiring streamlined shape.

Description—adults: All species are relatively small, with a maximum size of 64 mm. Males are smaller than females 20–50 mm versus 25–64 mm. Most species have rather slender, elongate bodies and relatively long legs. The snout usually projects beyond the mouth. The eyes are large, their diameter equal to or longer than the snout. The small eardrum

67

is visible. The tips of fingers and toes are usually rounded, but the outer fingers have slightly widened tips in several species. Webbing of the toes varies greatly among species. All species have rough skin, most species being covered with small, rounded warts. There are no enlarged parotoid glands behind the eye and above the eardrum. Colouration is usually brown or black, with indistinct pattern.

Tadpoles: Tadpoles of all species are small (mostly less than 20 mm) and have flattened bodies and cup-shaped lips forming a sucker. All but one (*A. leptopus*) have distinctly stream-lined bodies. The usual colouration is black.

Only a few species are likely to be encountered. We present notes on distinctive features of those species.

Ansonia albomaculata Inger
White-Lipped Slender Toad (Fig. 28)

Description: A stocky, small species, with snout projecting beyond mouth. The tips of all fingers are rounded, and the first finger is distinctly shorter than the second. The toes are almost fully webbed and the tips are rounded. This toad is reddish brown above, usually with a thin dark X over the shoulders. A slanting light band runs from the corner of the eye to the arm pit. There is often a light spot below the eye.
Males: 20–28 mm.
Females: 30–35 mm.

Tadpoles: The tadpoles are teardrop-shaped, small (maximum length 15 mm), and black with a light cross on the head and body.

Habits and habitat: This is a primary rain forest species, occurring below 900 metres above sea level. Adults move to the banks of medium-sized to large, clear, swift streams to breed. Calling males are found scattered along stream banks, but calling groups have not been seen. So far tadpoles have been found only in large streams.

Call: Unknown.

Fig. 28. *Ansonia albomaculata* Inger.

Distribution: Known from Brunei, Kalimantan, and Sarawak, but not Sabah.

Ansonia hanitschii Inger
Kinabalu Slender Toad (Fig. 29)

Description: A small slender, somewhat flat-bodied toad with a projecting snout. The toes are about three-fourths webbed and have rounded tips. The tips of the outer fingers are slightly widened, and the first finger is definitely shorter than the second. The back is covered with small rounded and a few oval warts; usually a few warts form short, slender ridges over the shoulders. These toads are dark greenish gray to reddish brown, often with black diagonal bars or spots on the back. The limbs have black crossbars.
Males: 20–28 mm
Females: 28–35 mm.

Tadpoles: Tadpoles are black and teardrop shaped. Maximum length is 20 mm.

Habits and habitats: This species lives in forests of mountainous country, at elevations higher than 950 metres above sea level. They are most often seen on the banks of small, rocky mountain creeks. Occasionally, large numbers of males are heard calling.

Call: a high-pitched chirp or short trill.

Distribution: So far this species has been found only in the mountains of western Sabah and northern Sarawak.

C.L. Chan

Fig. 29. *Ansonia hanitschii* Inger.

Ansonia leptopus (Günther)
Brown Slender Toad (Fig. 30)

Description: A slender-bodied species with long, thin hind legs. The toes are about three-fourths webbed in males, slightly less than that in females. The fingers have rounded tips like those of the toes. The entire back, sides, and upper surfaces of the limbs are rough, with many small, rounded warts. The top of the head usually has low ridges. Males have a single row of small orange or brown spines under the chin. This toad is uniformly brown on the back and top of the head, and slightly darker on

70

the sides. The underside of the head is dark gray with a brownish tinge, and the chest and belly are gray with darker mottling.
Males: 30–40 mm.
Females: 45–65 mm.

Tadpoles: The tadpoles are small (not more than 10 mm long) and light-bodied, with a black cross on the upper surface.

Habits and habitat: This is a toad of hilly primary forest or old secondary growth below 600 metres above sea level. Adults move to clear, medium-sized streams for breeding. Males usually call in groups from stream banks or from rocky bars in mid-stream. Tadpoles live mainly in accumulations of dead leaves in medium-sized clear streams often in association with tadpoles of *Rana signata, Rana leporina,* and *Pedostibes hosii.*

Call: A high pitched trill.

Distribution: Widely distributed in Borneo in hilly, but not mountainous country. Also known from Peninsular Malaysia.

Fig. 30. *Ansonia leptopus* (Günther).

71

Ansonia longidigita Inger
Long-Fingered Slender Toad (Fig. 31)

Description: A toad with long hind limbs. The snout projects beyond the mouth. The toes are about half webbed. The fingers have rounded tips like the toes. The first finger is at least as long as the second. Some of the warts on the upper surface of the body, especially those at the shoulder, are capped with small spines. Adult males have three or four rows of black, conical spines under the chin. This toad is clay brown to black. The limbs have dark crossbars on a clay brown background. The belly is cream-coloured, heavily spotted with brown or black.
Males: 35–50 mm.
Females: 45–70 mm.

Tadpoles: Tadpoles are black, teardrop shaped, and about 20–25 mm long.

R.F. Inger

Fig. 31. *Ansonia longidigita* Inger.

Habits and habitat: This toad lives in primary and old secondary or selectively logged forests in hilly or mountainous country from 150 to 2200 metres above sea level. Adults move to clear, swift, rocky streams to breed. Males form loose calling aggregations. Tadpoles are most often seen on large smooth rocks having a strong laminar flow. They are frequently found with tadpoles of Torrent Frogs (genus *Meristogenys*).

Call: A long, high-pitched trill.

Distribution: This species has been found in the western and central parts of Sabah, in Brunei, and many places in Sarawak. Though not yet reported from Kalimantan, it almost certainly will be found there. It has never been seen outside of Borneo.

Ansonia minuta Inger
Dwarf Slender Toad

Description: A small slender species with long hind limbs and snout projecting well beyond mouth. Tips of outer fingers are widened. The first finger is distinctly shorter than the second. Toes fully webbed in males, about three-fourths webbed in females. The upper surfaces of body and limbs covered with small, round warts. Adult males have two or three rows of yellowish spines under the chin. This toad is brown with irregular small orange or yellow spots or streaks on the back. The belly is pale with black spots and yellowish dots. The side of the head has dark and light bars, with a whitish area below the eye.
Males: 20–23 mm.
Females: 23–28 mm.

Tadpole: Unknown.

Habits and habitat: Little is known of this species except that it lives in hilly, lowland rain forest below 700 metres above sea level.

Call: Unknown.

Distribution: Found so far only in Sarawak and Kalimantan.

Ansonia spinulifer (Mocquard)
Spiny Slender Toad (Fig. 32)

Description: A comparatively slender species with the snout projecting slightly beyond the mouth. Tips of all fingers and toes are rounded, and the toes are almost free of webbing. The first finger is as long as the second. The entire back and hind legs are covered with conspicuous, large, spiny warts, which can easily be felt. The top of the head and body is black with a yellowish oval or diamond-shaped patch between the shoulders and a light streak along the side of the body. The belly is black with small cream-coloured spots or cream-coloured with heavy black marbling.
Males: 30–40 mm.
Females: 40–45 mm.

Tadpoles: Tadpoles are teardrop-shaped, black, and do not exceed 20 mm in length.

Habits and habitat: This toad has been seen perched on shrubs and herbs only along swift flowing, clear, rocky streams in primary forest below 700 metres above sea level. Males do not form calling groups.

Fig. 32. *Ansonia spinulifer* (Mocquard).

74

Tadpoles cling to large rocks in strong currents and feed on the film of algae growing on the rocks.

Call: Unknown.

Distribution: Known from all hilly parts of lowland Borneo wherever suitable environment exists. Not known outside of Borneo.

Genus *Bufo*
Toads

These are the so-called "true toads," frogs with warty skin, a large parotoid gland behind the eye and above the eardrum, rather short hind limbs, and usually narrow bony crests on the head. Although the parotoid gland and warts secrete a milky, latex-like toxin, it is not dangerous to handle these animals as long as one washes one's hands afterwards. The poison, however, is dangerous to small mammals, such as cats, that might try to prey on toads. The Bornean species of toads, like those elsewhere in the world, are terrestrial, although occasionally the Giant River Toad (*Bufo juxtasper*) may climb up a sloping dead tree. Diets of all species are similar: although they eat a great variety of insects and other invertebrates, the principal food is ants. With one exception (*B. melanostictus*), the Bornean species live in primary or secondary forests. *Bufo melanostictus* is a camp follower of mankind, living in environments created by humans—villages, towns, roadsides—and appears to be a recent invader of Borneo.

Bufo asper Gravenhorst
River Toad (Fig. 33)

Description: This is a large toad, with typical toad-like rough, warty skin. There are no bony crests on the head. The eardrum is visible. The parotoid gland behind the eye is usually round or oval, but the length is always less than twice the width. All the toes except the fourth (the longest) are webbed to the tips. The general colouration is dark brown or black.

Males: 70–100 mm.
Females: 95–140 mm.

Tadpole: The tadpoles are small (12–15 mm before metamorphosis) and black. The body is oval and slightly flattened, and the tail is shaped like a narrow leaf with a rounded tip. The lower lip is very wide.

Habits and habitat: This species lives in primary and old secondary forest in the lowlands. It is unlike most toads in that juveniles and adults do not wander through the forest but remain along stream banks. Adults do not move much, so that one may see the same individual toad sitting in the same spot on a stream bank for months. The tadpoles also differ from the usual toad pattern, living in strong currents and apparently clinging to the bottom with the enlarged lip.

Call: A raspy, chirp, sometimes repeated.

Distribution: Widely distributed in Sarawak, Brunei, and Kalimantan. In Sabah it appears to have a patchy distribution, having been found at only three or four scattered localities. Outside of Borneo, this species occurs in Java, Sumatra, and the Malay Peninsula.

R.F. Inger

Fig. 33. *Bufo asper* Gravenhorst.

Bufo juxtasper Inger
Giant River Toad (Fig. 34)

Description: This is a very large toad, with a broad, blunt head and typical toad-like warty skin. Like *B. asper*, it has no bony crests on the head. The eardrum is visible. The parotoid gland behind the eye is long, usually 2–4 times as long as wide, and often is tapered towards the rear. All the toes except the fourth (the longest) are webbed to the tips. The general colouration is dark gray, brown, or black, sometimes with obscure darker spots on the back. In addition to its large size, this species is remarkable for its bad, almost disgusting, smell.

Males: 90–120 mm.

Females: 125–215 mm.

R.B. Stuebing

Fig. 34. *Bufo juxtasper* Inger.

Tadpole: In general form and lips, this tadpole is like that of *B. asper*. The main differences are in size and colouration. Just before metamorphosis the tadpoles of *B. juxtasper* measure 15–20 mm. The underside of the head in *B. juxtasper* tadpoles is dark; in tadpoles of *B. asper* the underside of the head is white or pink.

77

Habits and habitat: *Bufo juxtasper* can be found wandering through primary and old secondary forest from near sea level to 1600 metres. This species is not as tied to stream banks as is *B. asper*. However, these two species are alike in breeding site and habitat of tadpoles. *Bufo juxtasper* seems to breed in swifter currents than *B. asper*, and we have found tadpoles of *B. juxtasper* in strong rapids.

Call: A hoarse, squeaky croak or chirp. In Sabah, the Dusun name for this species is "bu'angkut," which imitates the sound of not one, but two toads calling at night. Frequently toads of two different sizes (and, thus, tones of voice) will sit within several metres of one another. When the first calls, the other rapidly answers, resulting in a two-syllable sound that appears to originate from one caller.

Distribution: Known from all parts of Borneo. The distribution in Sarawak is spotty, while in Sabah this toad is extremely abundant in the lowlands.

Bufo divergens Peters
Crested Toad (Fig. 35)

Description: A small stocky toad, with many scattered, spiny warts on the back and sides. The snout is narrow and projects beyond the mouth. There is a pair of narrow, raised crests between the eyes. The eardrum is visible. The parotoid gland behind the eye is longer than wide, tapered toward the rear, and is usually followed by a oblique row of warts. The length of the gland is less than three times its width. None of the toes is fully webbed. The general colour is clay to reddish brown, often with a series of black chevrons on the back.
Males: 28–43 mm.
Females: 36–55 mm.

Tadpole: The tadpoles are oval, black and small. Just before metamorphosis, they are 15–17 mm long. These are typical toad tadpoles. They do not have expanded lips like tadpoles of *B. asper* and *B. juxtasper*.

Habits and habitat: This is a toad of forest floor leaf litter. It occurs in

Fig. 35. *Bufo divergens* Peters.

primary and old secondary forest below 700 metres above sea level. Adults breed at very shallow, small streams or in rain pools on the forest floor. Males usually form noisy calling groups. Tadpoles from eggs laid in small streams usually are found where the current is weakest.

Call: A querulous, raspy, rising trill.

Distribution: Found throughout Borneo. Elsewhere it is known from Sumatra.

Bufo quadriporcatus Boulenger
Swamp Toad (Fig. 36)

Description: This is a small to medium-sized, stocky toad with a pair of short, raised ridges between the eyes, as in *B. divergens*. The snout is narrow and projects beyond the mouth. The eardrum is visible. The parotoid gland is long, compressed from side to side, and distinctly raised. It is more than three times as long as wide and ends in a row of large, spiny warts. The back has low, smooth warts, whereas the sides have many small, spiny warts. None of the toes are fully webbed. The colour is dark brown to almost black, usually without markings.

Males: 48–50 mm.

Females: 49–62 mm.

Tadpole: Unknown, but probably very similar to that of the related *B. divergens*.

Habits and habitat: This species seems to be confined to swampy forests near the coast. It is very abundant in such environments but has not been seen in hilly country. It almost surely breeds in the pools of standing water that are so common in swamps.

Call: Unknown.

Distribution: This species has been reported from Kalimantan, Sabah, and Sarawak. It probably also occurs in Brunei, which has large areas of appropriate environment. This species also occurs in Sumatra and Peninsular Malaysia.

R.F. Inger

Fig. 36. *Bufo quadriporcatus* Boulenger.

Bufo melanostictus Schneider
Common Sunda Toad (Fig. 37)

Description: A stocky, medium-sized to large toad with a relatively small head and short hind limbs. Long dark crests border the eyelids and run down on either side of the eye. Another, thicker crest runs from the eye to the parotoid gland. The gland is large, oval, and about as long as eye and snout combined. The back is covered with round warts of varying sizes, often surrounded by darker pigment and capped with tiny dark spines. The general colour is grayish or reddish brown, usually without markings except for the warty areas.

Males: 57–83 mm.

Females: 65–85 mm.

Tadpole: Shaped like tadpoles of *B. divergens*. Black and small, not over 15 mm long.

Habits and habitat: As already mentioned, this is the only Bornean toad that does not live in forests. It has adapted to the environmental disturbances created by mankind and occurs throughtout tropical Asia in

Fig. 37. *Bufo melanostictus* Schneider.

villages and towns. Adults are usually found either at temporary rain pools or drains, or under street lamps where they feed on the insects dropping from the lights. Tadpoles develop in standing water.

Call: A low rattling trill.

Distribution: Known from towns in Sarawak and Kalimantan. It has been found so far only in one small village near Kota Kinabalu in western Sabah.

Leptophryne borbonica (Tschudi)
Cross Toad (Fig. 38)

Description: A small slender bodied toad with long legs and a short, tapered snout which projects slightly over the mouth in profile. The eardrum is oval, and about one-third the size of the eye. There is no paratoid gland, or any distinct enlarged glands over the upper sides of the

Fig. 38. *Leptophryne borbonica* (Tschudi).

82

body, except for a slightly raised fold of skin that runs down the sides of the back. The tips of the fingers and toes are rounded and blunt. Webbing is restricted to the base of the toes. The colour is grayish with brown markings, usually forming an X in the middle of the back. The throat and chest are dark brown, while the belly is gray to yellowish. The undersides of the legs are also grayish or yellowish with brown spots.

Males: 27–31

Females: 40–47

Tadpoles: Unknown.

Habits and habitat: These small toads are most often found in the leaf litter of seepage areas in forests below 400 metres above sea level.

Call: Not recorded.

Distribution: Known from all parts of Borneo. The species also occurs in southeastern Asia and Sumatra.

Genus *Pedostibes*

This long-legged group of medium to large-sized forest toads are probably the only truly arboreal members of the Bufonidae. They occur mostly in undisturbed forests, though they may be encountered in old secondary habitats. Their fingers are long and distinctly shaped, probably an adaptation to climbing. Some individuals of the brown tree toad, *Pedostibes hosii*, have been found as high as six metres up in trees. The only tadpoles known are of this species, occurring in accumulations of dead leaves in the quiet side pools of forest streams. Adult frogs of this genus eat a diet which is mostly ants.

Pedostibes hosii (Boulenger)
Brown Tree Toad (Fig. 39)

Description: A large, stout toad with a thick bony ridge behind the eye connected to a small parotoid gland. The eardrum is visible. The toes, except for the fourth (longest), are completely webbed, and the tips are slightly widened. The finger tips are expanded into stubby pads, and there is a slight webbing at the bases of the fingers. The top of the head is smooth, and the back has a few scattered warts. All males and about half of the females are uniform light to chocolate brown. The remainder of the females are black or dark purple with a pattern of yellow spots forming a dense network.

Males: 53–78 mm.

Females: 89–105 mm.

Fig. 39. *Pedostibes hosii* (Boulenger).

Tadpole: The body is oval and the tail is shaped like a narrow leaf with a rounded tip. The colour is dark brown above and on the sides, without markings. Total length reaches 19–20 mm.

Habits and habitat: This arboreal toad lives in primary forest in lowlands below 600 metres above sea level. Adults come to medium-sized, clear streams to breed. Breeding is not seasonal, but occurs in spurts or pulses with many individuals coming to breed for one or two nights, then retiring to the forest for several weeks. The males do not form calling aggregations, but some nights there are so many present that they seem to be every where along the bank. Adults feed on a variety of insects, with ants being the dominant component. The tadpoles live in quiet side pools and in masses of dead leaves on the bottoms of streams.

Call: A grating, slurred squawk, rising in pitch slightly from beginning to end.

Distribution: All parts of Borneo. The species is also known from Sumatra, Peninsular Malaysia, and southern Thailand.

Pedostibes rugosus Inger
Marbled Tree Toad (Fig. 40)

Description: A medium-sized, stout toad, with extremely rough, warty skin and a large egg-shaped parotoid gland behind the eye. The eardrum is visible. The tips of the fingers are slightly widened, but blunt. All the toes, except the fourth (the longest), are fully webbed. The colour is bright green with brown or reddish brown spots. Front and hind legs have broad brown cross bars.
Males: 74–77 mm.
Females: 80–95 mm.

Tadpole: Unknown.

Habits and habitat: This species has been found only in hilly primary forest from 150 to 1050 metres above sea level. We suspect that adults are arboreal and disperse through the forest. All the adults we have seen have been caught at breeding sites along clear, rocky streams.

Call: Unknown.

Distribution: Known from Sabah, Sarawak, and western Kalimantan. Presumably, this species occurs throughout Borneo. It is not known from elsewhere.

Fig. 40. *Pedostibes rugosus* Inger.

Genus *Pelophryne*
Dwarf Toads

These are small toads with small, scattered warts on the back and head, but without a large parotoid gland behind the eye. All have the fingers partly webbed. Because they have not been observed very often, very little is known of their natural history. Females of all species have very small clutches (less than 20) of large, whitish eggs. Tadpoles of one

86

species were found in a shallow pool; they clearly were not feeding, as they lacked the usual larval mouth parts, and were completing development based on the large amount of yolk contained in the egg.

Species of *Pelophryne* have never been seen outside of primary or old secondary forest, and are known to occur from near sea level to 3100 metres. Most individuals have been found on the forest floor, but they also climb into low vegetation.

Pelophryne misera (Mocquard)
Kinabalu Dwarf Toad (Fig. 41)

Description: A very small toad, with the hand webbed, including the entire first finger and half of the outer fingers. The tips of the fingers are narrow. Webbing on the foot reaches the tips of the first three toes. The eardrum is visible. The back and sides have small, scattered, round or oval warts. The colour is black or dark brown, with white blotches on the underside.

Fig. 41. *Pelophryne misera* (Mocquard).

Males: 16–21 mm.
Females: 18–23 mm.

Tadpole: Unknown, but probably as described under genus.

Habits and habitat: All known records of this species are from elevations between 1600 and 3100 metres above sea level in mossy montane forest. This species has been seen mostly at ground level, but two adults were found in the cup of a pitcher plant on Mount Kinabalu. Females have clutches of 6–16 eggs.

Call: Unknown.

Distribution: Mount Kinabalu, Sabah. There is one report from Mount Murud, Sarawak. Probably the species occurs on other mountains in Borneo.

Pelophryne rhopophilius Inger & Stuebing
Climbing Dwarf Toad (Fig. 42)

Description: A very small toad, with thick webbing on the hand reaching the ends of the two inner fingers but only the bases of the two outer ones. The tips of the fingers are widened into blunt pads. Thick webbing on the foot leaves just the tips of the three inner toes free. The eardrum is visible. The back has many small, round warts, each of which has a tiny whitish cone in the centre. The back is brown or black, often with dark markings outlining a broad X. The underside of the body is white with small black spots that occupy less than half the total area.
Males: 21–24 mm.
Females: 23 mm.

Tadpole: Unknown.

Habits and habitat: This species has been collected just twice. On one occasion, six males were calling from leaves of bushes in a submontane forest at 815 metres above sea level.

Call: Unknown.

Distribution: Known only from southeastern Sarawak and neighboring western Kalimantan.

Fig. 42. *Pelophryne rhopophilius* Inger & Stuebing.

Pelophryne signata (Boulenger)
Lowland Dwarf Toad (Fig. 43)

Description: A remarkably tiny toad, with thick webbing on the hand reaching the tip of the first finger but leaving half of the outer fingers free. The tips of the fingers are widened into blunt disks. Thick webbing on the foot reaches the tips of the first two toes only. The eardrum is visible. The back has small, round warts. The back is black or dark brown with small black spots. Some individuals have a wide, dark X-shaped mark on the back. There is a yellow or cream-coloured band from below the eye passing above the armpit to the side.
Male: 14–17 mm.
Female: 16–18 mm.

Tadpole: Unknown, but presumably as described under the genus.

Habits and habitat: This species lives in flat or hilly primary forest from near sea level to about 1000 metres. We have found it on the ground and in low vegetation. Females have small clutches of large eggs that are about one-tenth the length of the body.

Call: Unknown.

Distribution: All parts of Borneo. This species has also been reported from the Bunguran Islands and Peninsular Malaysia.

Fig. 43. *Pelophryne signata* (Boulenger).

Pseudobufo subasper Tschudi
Aquatic swamp toad (Fig. 44)

Description: A large, stocky toad with a small head, and nostrils on the top of the snout. The fingers are long, slender and blunt, with slight webbing at the bases. The toes are fully webbed to the tips. The back is covered with large, round warts, and there are distinct parotoid glands. The back and sides are brown, with a yellowish to yellow-orange stripe along where back and sides meet. The belly is yellowish, while in mature

90

Kelvin Lim

Fig. 44. *Pseudobufo subasper* Tschudi.

females the throat is yellowish and in males, black.
Males: 77–94 mm.
Females: 92–155 mm.

Tadpole: Unknown.

Habits and habitat: Adults are usually found in pools among the floating vegetation mainly in coastal and peat swamps associated with large rivers (such as the Kapuas in Kalimantan). The cryptic colouration and lethargic habits of this toad make it difficult to find. Males have been reported to call from mats of vegetation overhanging water, into which they promptly dive if disturbed.

Call: Unknown.

Distribution: The only Bornean specimens have been found in Kalimantan. The species is also known from Sumatra and Peninsular Malaysia.

CHAPTER 9

FAMILY MICROHYLIDAE
(NARROW-MOUTHED FROGS)

This family is essentially tropical in its distribution with only a few species living in temperate climates.

Genus *Calluella*
Spadefoot Frogs

All the frogs of this group are burrowers and, because of that, the Bornean species are rarely seen. Only one species has been collected more than three times, and one species is known from a single specimen. Nothing is known about the breeding habits of the Bornean species, but those from Thailand and other parts of the continent breed in small temporary ponds.

Description - adults: All of these frogs have rather flat bodies, wide heads, hidden eardrums, and small eyes for frogs. The tips of the fingers and toes are not widened and the toes have very little webbing. All of them have a large compressed flange under the foot, which besides being the reason for the common name is the structure used in digging.

Tadpoles: The tadpoles of the Bornean species are unknown.

Calluella brooksi (Boulenger)
Brooks' Spadefoot Frog

Description: A medium-sized, stocky frog with an extremely broad, short head and short, thick legs. The snout is stubby, with the nostrils at

its very end. The toes are narrowly webbed at the base. All of the upper surfaces are medium brown, with many scattered, small black spots. The throat of males is black, that of females whitish. The chest and abdomen are whitish or yellowish.
Males: 51–55 mm.
Female: 60 mm.

Tadpole: Unknown.

Habits and habitat: There is little known about this species other than its burrowing habits. All records are from forests at elevations close to sea level.

Call: Unknown.

Distribution: Recorded from Kalimantan and Sarawak.

Calluella smithi (Barbour & Noble)
Blotch-Sided Spadefoot Frog

Description: A small stocky frog with a wide head and short, thick legs. The snout is narrowed above the jaw, with the nostrils near the tip. The toes are narrowly webbed at the base. The skin of the back and top of the head is smooth with a few scattered, round bumps. The throat of the male is finely granular and the belly of both sexes is smooth or finely pebbled. The back and top of the head are tan or medium brown. The sides are a lighter tan or yellowish, with a finger of the lighter colour projection up onto the back. The lower sides and hidden surfaces of the legs have large black blotches, each of which has a narrow red border. The throat of the male is black, while that of the female is brown with several yellowish spots. The abdomen is yellowish with brown spots or mottling around the margins.
Male: 33 mm.
Females: 38–40 mm.

Tadpole: Unknown.

Habits and habitat: This species is known from primary forests at low elevations. They have sometimes been found under dead leaves or logs on the forest floor.

Call: Unknown.

Distribution: Recorded only from Sabah and Sarawak.

Chaperina fusca Mocquard
Saffron-Bellied Frog (Fig. 45)

Description: A very small frog with a body the size and shape of a large almond. The tips of the fingers and toes ared slightly widened, and athe toes have no webbing. There is a tiny flexible spine at the elbow and heel. The back is greenish black, while the underside of the body and legs has a black network enclosing bright yellow spots. Oddly, the yellow colour will rub off onto human fingers quite easily.
Males: 18–21 mm.
Females: 20–24 mm.

R.B. Stuebing

Fig. 45. *Chaperina fusca* Mocquard.

Tadpole: These are small, oval, and slightly flattened above. The tail tapers abruptly near the end to a rounded tip. The body is black above, lighter below. The tail fins are colourless. Total length reaches 20 mm.

Habits and habitat: This species lives in primary and secondary forest and will even live in gardens. It is especially abundant in flat country, but also occurs in hills. Although this species is essentially an inhabitant of the forest floor, it sometimes climbs into low vegetation. Males form calling groups around small, temporary pools of water. Eggs may be laid in clear or turbid water, sometimes in water that is rank with decaying matter. The tadpoles hover in mid-water, filtering microorganisms.

Call: A short, insect-like buzz.

Distribution: Occurs in all parts of Borneo. It also is found in the southern Philippine Islands and Peninsular Malaysia.

Genus *Kalophrynus*
Sticky Frogs

Kalophrynus are small to tiny sticky frogs of the leaf litter with pointed noses and short, slender hind legs. Three have spots in the groin (inside the thigh). Their habits are quite similar. All live in the forest floor litter where they feed mainly on ants and termites.

Kalophrynus baluensis Kiew
Kinabalu Sticky Frog (Fig. 46)

Description: A small, stocky frog, with a relatively narrow head, pointed snout, and short, slender hind legs. Fingers and toes are not webbed, and the fingers are long, with slightly flattened, blunt tips. The eardrum is not visible. The skin is finely granular, with a raised fold across the head between the eyes. The head is brown, and the back is brownish with irregular light patches. The sides of the head are yellowish with dark spots, while the sides of the body are light brown.

96

Fig. 46. *Kalophrynus baluensis* Kiew.

There is a dark brown spot running from the snout to the groin on each side of the back. The belly is grayish white with scattered brown spots and enlarged whitish bumps.
Males: 36 mm.
Females: 39 mm.

Tadpole: Unknown.

Habits and habitat: This is a frog of the leaf litter known only from primary montane forest on Mount Kinabalu at about 1500 metres. When handled, it exudes a sticky mucus. Its habits are probably somewhat similar to those of the better known *K. pleurostigma*. Males call after heavy rains and breed in temporary pools.

Call: Unknown.

Distribution: Known only from Mount Kinabalu in Sabah. It probably also occurs on the higher mountains in Sarawak and Kalimantan.

Kalophrynus heterochirus Boulenger
Variable Sticky Frog (Fig. 47)

Description: A small, stocky frog, with a narrow head, pointed snout, and slender hind legs. The outermost toe and finger are very short, and the toes have little webbing. The skin is finely granular, and glistens slightly when the frog is handled. Adults are rusty orange to dark brown above, with similarly coloured sides separated by a fine, dark-bordered light line running diagonally from the snout to the groin. From one to several dark-bordered cream-coloured spots may occur both in the groin area and on the inner thigh of each hind leg, becoming conspicuous when the frog jumps. The throat and chest are creamy white with dark markings.
Males: 24–27 mm.
Females: 30–33 mm.

Tadpole: Unknown.

Habits and habitat: This is a frog of the leaf litter known from primary and secondary forest from near sea level to 1200 metres. Like other *Kalophrynus* it exudes a sticky, glue-like mucus from glands in the skin of the back The calling sites of males are probably small, temporary

Fig. 47. *Kalophrynus heterochirus* Boulenger.

pools on the forest floor, or in rotting logs. Juveniles and adults feed on tiny invertebrates, such as small species of ants and termites.

Call: Unknown.

Distribution: Sabah, Sarawak, and Kalimantan.

Kalophrynus intermedius Inger
Intermediate Sticky Frog (Fig. 48)

Description: A small frog, with a narrow head, rounded snout, and short limbs. The outermost toe and finger are very short, and the toes have little webbing. The skin is coarsely granular, with a disinct gland behind the ear. Adults are brown above, sometimes with obscure dark markings on the back. The sides are yellowish to cream-coloured, meeting at a sharp boundary with the colouration of the back. The throat has two irregular, dark longitudinal bands. The throat is pinkish, while the chest and belly are cream-coloured. There are a few dark spots on the abdomen near the chest.
Males: 27 mm.
Females: 38–41 mm.

Fig. 48. *Kalophrynus intermedius* Inger.

Tadpole: Unknown.

Habits and habitat: This is a frog of the leaf litter known from lowland primary forest below 300 metres elevation, and only from Sarawak.

Call: Unknown

Distribution: Sarawak. Like other small, secretive species in this genus, this species probably occurs in other parts of Borneo.

Kalophrynus pleurostigma Tschudi
Rufous-sided Sticky Frog (Fig. 49)

Description: A small, stocky frog, with a relatively narrow head and pointed snout, resulting in a somewhat triangular shape. The outermost toe and finger are very short, and the toes have little webbing. Females have a finely pebbled upper surface, while males have many tiny spines. Frogs are light to dark brown above, with rusty-orange sides, separated by a fine, whitish line running diagonally from the snout to the groin. A black spot is conspicuous just in front of each hind leg. The throat and chest are rusty to brownish and the abdomen light gray to gray.
Males: 37–50 mm.
Females: 35–57 mm.

Tadpole: Gray to olive tadpoles with an egg-shaped body and tail ending in a blunt tip. These small (maximum total length about 9 mm) tadpoles apparently do not feed, but complete their development using the yolk present in the egg.

Habits and habitat: This is a frog of the leaf litter known only from primary forest at low elevations. When handled, its skin exudes a sticky, glue-like mucus from glands in the skin of the back The calling sites of males are near small, shallow temporary pools on the forest floor, or in rotting logs. Tadpoles have been found in very small, shallow pools of water, such as crevices of logs. Juveniles and adults feed on ants and termites. The frog moves until it finds an ant or termite trail or nest, then laps up the prey until satisfied. We have found over one hundred ants in a single stomach.

Fig. 49. *Kalophrynus pleurostigma* Tschudi.

Call: Probably a sharp, repetitive chirp.

Disribution: Found in all parts of Borneo. It also occurs in Peninsular Malaysia, Sumatra, and the southern Philippine Islands.

Kalophrynus subterrestris Inger
Lesser Sticky Frog (Fig. 50)

Description: A small to tiny frog, with a narrow head, rounded snout, and short limbs. The outer most toe and finger are very short, and the toes have little webbing. The skin is coarsely granular, and glistens slightly when the frog is handled.

Adults are brown above, with slightly darker coloured sides, separated by a fine, light line running diagonally from the snout to the groin. The throat and chest are dusky with light spots or pale yellowish with a dark band under the jaw.

101

R.F. Inger

Fig. 50 (above). *Kalophrynus subterrestris* Inger. **Fig. 51** (below). *Kaloula baleata* (Müller).

R.B. Stuebing

Tadpoles: Unknown.

Habits and habitat: This is a frog of the leaf litter known from primary and old secondary forest of the lowlands. Males have been collected calling at the entrance to burrows. Juveniles and adults feed on tiny invertebrates, such as small species of ants and termites.

Call: Unknown.

Distribution: Known from Sabah and Sarawak. This secretive species probably also occurs in Brunei and Kalimantan.

Kaloula baleata (Müller)
Brown Bullfrog (Fig. 51)

Description: A squat, round frog with short, thick hind limbs and a short snout. The eardrum is not visible. The tips of the fingers are widened and blunt. The toes have only slight webbing and are blunt at the tips. The sole of the foot has a pair of prominent ridges or flanges at the base of the toes. The skin is finely granular, often with scattered lumps. Colour of the back varies from chocolate to dark brown, often with a lighter band from behind the eye over the shoulder to the elbow. The rump is darker than the fore part of the back.
Males: 50–61 mm.
Females: 55–66 mm.

Tadpole: Eggs are laid in the rain pools formed in the depressions of the disturbed habitats where these frogs live. Tadpoles are grayish brown with an unpigmented tail, with their eyes on the sides of the head. Maximum length is about 25 mm.

Habits and habitat: This frog prefers disturbed or secondary habitats inland, such as the flood plains of rivers, or ponds and ditches produced by logging or agricultural activities. It apparently secrets itself in plant debris such as dry leaves during dry periods, emerging rapidly and in large numbers to breed after a extended heavy rains. It forms large noisy breeding groups, calling loudly from hidden sites in vegetation. During a call, males inflate themselves grotesquely. The diet is mostly ants, though other small crawling insects are also eaten.

Call: A loud sharp honk.

Kaloula pulchra (Gray)
Banded Bullfrog (Fig. 52)

Description: A squat, round frog with short, thick hind legs and a short rounded snout. The toes have only a small amount of webbing at the base, and are blunt at the tips. There is a prominent "spade" or flange on the sole of each foot between the heel and the base of the toes. The fingers are long, with no webbing, are but slightly widened, and are blunt at the tips.

The skin is finely pebbled, and there are widely scattered light coloured bumps over the lower back. The frogs are chocolate to dark brown with scattered dark spots. Two wide, irregular, tan coloured bands run backwards from the eye to the groin. In most individuals a row of dark spots forms a line down the centre of the back from the top of the head to the anus. The snout in front of the eyes is also tan in colour, while the undersides of the head are brown. The chest, belly and undersides of the legs have scattered brown spots, sometimes connected to form a network.
Males: 54–67 mm
Females: 55–75 mm

Tadpoles: Eggs are laid in the temporary pools where the frogs call. The tadpoles are blackish with transparent fins, and their eyes are set on the sides of the head. Maximum length is about 25 mm.

Habits and habitat: This is a frog of human settlements, primarily of towns and cities. It lives under rubbish heaps and other accumulated debris (such as in clogged drains) during dry periods, emerging in vast numbers after downpours of several hours or more. It forms large noisy

Fig. 52 (Opposite). *Kaloula pulchra* (Gray).

breeding groups in flooded areas such as flooded drainage systems or lawns. Males inflate themselves in a grotesque manner as they call while floating at the surface of these temporary ponds. *Kaloula pulchra* eats almost exclusively ants, though it will occasionally take small beetles or other crawling insects.

Call: A loud groaning honk.

Distribution: Reported from Sarawak and western Sabah. This is a relatively recent introduction into Borneo, probably by accident rather than deliberately. It is not known how far it has spread in Borneo. The species is widely distributed in tropical Asia.

R.B. Stuebing

Metaphrynella sundana (Peters)
Tree Hole Frog (Fig. 53)

Description: A tiny, stocky frog with a pointed snout. The tips of the fingers are widened and the underside of each finger has a thickened, fleshy pad at the base. The feet are rather fleshy and the toes are about half webbed. The back and tops of the legs are covered with minute warts. The frogs are gray or light brown, usually with a large dark brown mark down the centre of the back. The tops of the fingers are yellow.
Males: 19–23 mm.
Females: 23–25 mm.

Tadpole: Unknown.

Habits and habitat: This is an abundant species of flat and hilly primary forest of the lowlands. Males call from water-containing holes in small trees, usually between one and three metres above ground. Females move about, apparently going to a hole from which a male calls when she is ready to breed. The piping calls of this species is one of the characteristic night sounds of forests below 700 metres.

R.B. Stuebing

Fig. 53. *Metaphrynella sundana* (Peters).

Call: A single piping note at regular intervals. The tone varies, indicating that dimensions of the hole affect the pitch.

Distribution: All parts of Borneo. It is not known elsewhere.

Genus *Microhyla*
Narrow-Mouthed Frogs

Five species of *Microhyla* are now known from Borneo. Only one species, *M. berdmorei*, occurs outside of Borneo. All five are small to tiny and have long hind limbs. They all live in primary and old secondary forests below 700 metres above sea level. Their generally brown colouration with a broken, dark pattern make them difficult to see on the leaf litter of the forest floor, and their capacity for long leaps makes them very difficult to catch. All species lay eggs in very small pools of water. Most species have a dark marking from between the eyes down the back; the dark area narrows and widens, usually sending pairs of dark arms backward and to the side.

Microhyla berdmorei (Blyth)
Berdmore's Narrow-Mouthed Frog (Fig. 54)

Description: A small frog, with long hind limbs. Eardrum not visible. Snout rather blunt. Four fingers evident. Tips of toes widened and all except fourth (longest) fully webbed to base of pads. Skin smooth. Colour light brown or gray brown, with dark brown mark in centre of back and between eyes. Usually a slanting dark brown band low on the side. The throat is brown and the belly white.
Males: 24–28 mm.
Females: 27–32 mm.

Tadpole: Unknown.

Habits and habitat: This species occurs in primary and secondary forests at low elevations. Like all members of this genus, adults live on the ground in leaf litter.

Fig. 54. *Microhyla berdmorei* (Blyth).

Call: Unknown.

Distribution: Known from a few localities in Sabah, Sarawak, and Kalimantan. It probably has a wide distribution in Borneo along major river valleys. The species is also known from Thailand, Peninsular Malaysia, and Sumatra.

Microhyla borneensis Parker
Bornean Narrow-Mouthed Frog (Fig. 55)

Description: A small frog with long hind limbs. Eardrum not visible. Snout slightly pointed and projecting beyond mouth. Four fingers evident. Tips of toes slightly widened. Three outer toes about half webbed. Skin smooth. This species is gray to brown on the back, with a wide, dark brown or purple, light-edged mark down the centre of the back. This dark mark has pairs of arms projecting backward and to the side. The chest and belly are mottled brown and white.

Males: 17–18 mm.

Females: 19–23 mm.

Tadpole: The head and body appear triangular, flat above and rounded below. The tail tapers gradually from its base into a long narrow filament. The entire tadpole is gray or black, except under the body. Total length reaches 22 mm.

Habits and habitat: This species is known only from primary forests in lowlands. Adults live on the forest floor and breed at small rain pools. We found several in wild pig wallows.

Call: Unknown.

Distribution: Reported so far only from Sarawak and Sabah. It will probably be found throughout the lowland forests of Borneo.

R.F. Inger

Fig. 55. *Microhyla borneensis* Parker.

Microhyla petrigena Inger & Frogner
Pothole Narrow-Mouthed Frog (Fig. 56)

Description: A very small species, with long hind legs. This and *M. perparva* are the only Bornean species of *Microhyla* that have just three fingers. The eardrum is not visible. The tips of the toes are widened and all toes except the fourth (longest) are fully webbed to the pads. The skin is smooth. The general colour is light gray-brown, with the top of the head slightly darker. A dark mark occupies the centre of the back, with three constrictions and expansions. The throat and belly are dark brown with an irregular, large, white blotch in the centre.
Males: 14–16 mm.
Females: 15–18 mm.

Fig. 56. *Microhyla petrigena* Inger & Frogner.

Tadpole: The head and body are oval, flattened above and rounded below. The tail is deep and tapered abruptly near the end to a short, narrow tip. The head and body are black above and on the sides. The tail fins are colourless except for a wide, vertical black band near the end. Total length reaches 15–17 mm.

Habits and habitat: This is a species of the floor litter in primary forests below 700 metres above sea level. Adults feed on tiny ants and other invertebrates. Breeding takes place at small potholes on rocky banks of

110

streams. The holes where tadpoles have been found were less than 30 cm in diameter and depth. The tadpoles hover at mid-depth in these tiny pools and filter tiny organisms from the water.

Call: Unknown.

Distribution: Sabah and Sarawak. There is no reason to believe that this species does not occur in Kalimantan and Brunei.

Microhyla perparva Inger & Frogner
Least Narrow-Mouthed Frog (Fig. 57)

Description: Very similar to *M. petrigena*. Only three fingers evident. Principal difference are in size and colouration. *Microhyla perparva* has a dusky throat, but the belly is entirely white.
Males: 10–12 mm.
Females: 13–15 mm.

Fig. 57. *Microhyla perparva* Inger & Frogner.

111

Tadpole: Head, body, and tail are shaped as in tadpole of *M. petrigena*. Colouration also similar to that of *M. petrigena*. Total length reaches 10–12 mm.

Habits and habitat: This species lives in flat or hilly primary forest at low elevations. Adults breed at rain pools in the forest.

Call: Unknown.

Distribution: This species has been found in Sarawak at several areas, but has been seen at only one site in Sabah. It probably also occurs in Kalimantan.

CHAPTER 10

FAMILY RANIDAE

This is probably the most familiar group of frogs; it occurs almost everywhere in the world and is the largest family in Borneo.

Hoplobatrachus rugulosus (Wiegmann)
Taiwanese Frog (Fig. 58)

Description: A large, powerfully built frog with a broad triangular head. The toes are fully webbed and rounded at the tips. The middle two fingers have a fringe of skin along the inner side, while the other fingers have no fringes. The tips of the fingers are pointed. The eardrum is large The skin is extremely granular and rough, with many scattered, small to large bumps along the sides of the back and rump. There are also many interrupted, prominent horny ridges of skin running down the back and upper surfaces of the calves. The sides are covered with densely packed conical bumps. These frogs are brown to greenish gray above, with scattered dark spots on the back and legs. The sides are spotted or mottled, forming a pattern or network in large individuals. The underside of the head is whitish with a distinct dark streak down the middle of the throat. Some individuals the throat is heavily mottled with dark spots forming a network. The chest is lightly spotted, and the belly and under surfaces of the legs usually white.
Males: 70–100 mm.
Females: 85–125 mm.

Tadpoles: The tadpoles of this species are large (up to 80 mm), and have heavy, sharp, black beaks. The body is very dark above, and somewhat lighter on the sides with irregular black spots.

Habits and habitat: This frog is not native to Borneo. It was apparently imported into Sabah from East Asia (possible Taiwan) in the 1960's as

113

Fig. 58. *Hoplobatrachus rugulosus* (Wiegmann).

Fig. 59. *Huia cavitympanum* (Boulenger).

source of meat. It has now spread throughout western Sabah from Kota Belud to Tenom and, perhaps, beyond. It seems to be limited to disturbed areas, from rice fields to construction sites. The frogs gather in breeding groups around temporary ponds, and males call from these areas of standing water after heavy storms. This species eats a wide variety of invertebrates and probably also preys on smaller frogs. In Southeast Asia, the tadpoles of this species are known to feed on small tadpoles. They almost certainly have the same habits in Borneo. Since most tadpoles of other species that live in disturbed environments also develop in temporary ponds, the predatory behaviour of *rugulosus* tadpoles may account for the success of this species as an invader.

Call: A low raspy note, repeated rapidly 10–20 times.

Distribution: In Borneo known only from western Sabah. The species occurs in open, disturbed environments throughout Southeast Asia.

Huia cavitympanum (Boulenger)
Hole-in-the-Head Frog (Fig. 59)

Description: A medium-sized to large frog, with a rounded snout and long hind limbs. The tips of the fingers and toes are expanded into slightly pointed pads. All toes are fully webbed to the base of the pads. This is the only species of frog in Borneo having the eardrum sunk into a depression. The skin is smooth except for small, round bumps on the sides and roughened areas on the sides of the head. The top of the head and the back are chocolate brown. The sides of the head and body and the upper surfaces of the limbs are tan with dark brown spots. Throat, chest and belly are white or yellowish orange. The upper half of the iris is light gold and the lower half cinnamon brown.
Males: 42–52 mm.
Females: 75–80 mm.

Tadpole: The tadpoles of this species are among the largest in Borneo, reaching a length of 70 mm. They have an abdominal sucker enabling them to cling to rocks in swift currents. The muscle of the tail is dark with light spots, and the fins are also dark but have a light band along the base and light spots along the margins.

Habits and habitat: This species lives in primary forest in hilly country from 250 to 750 metres above sea level. Adults wander widely through the forest, but it is not known whether they feed on the ground or climb up into vegetation. They breed only along stretches of swift water in medium-sized to large streams. The tadpoles live in the strongest currents on those streams, clinging to bedrock or boulders with their abdominal sucker.

Call: A weak, high-pitched chirp.

Distribution: Kalimantan, Sabah, and Sarawak. This species has never been found outside of Borneo.

Ingerana baluensis (Boulenger)
Dwarf Inger's Frog (Fig. 60)

Description: A very small, stocky frog with a wide, somewhat pointed head and short hind limbs. It has short, stubby fingers with broadened tips. The toes have widened tips and are about half webbed. The skin of the head and back is pebbled and often set with short, narrow ridges. The belly and throat also have a pebbled surface. Colouration is variable. Some individuals are medium brown with small, scattered dark spots on the back and dark bars between the nostrils and between the eyes. Other individuals are gray-brown on top of the snout and on the sides, but are dark brown on the back beginning between the eyes. In still others, the back has a dark longitudinal band with deeply indented margins. A few are dark brown except for a light streak on each side of the back. The chest and belly are pale gray or white. The throat is usually heavily dotted or marbled with brown.
.Males: 20–25 mm.
Females: 24–30 mm.

Tadpoles: Unknown.

Habits and habitat: Very little is known about this forest frog. All observed so far were seen on the forest floor or at the edges of streams, although the expanded tips of fingers and toes suggest that the species climbs.

Call: Unknown.

Distribution: Known only from Sabah and Sarawak.

Fig. 60. *Ingerana baluensis* (Boulenger).

Genus *Meristogenys*
Torrent Frogs

This is a uniquely Bornean group of frogs; no species of this genus has been found anywhere else. As a group, adults of *Meristogenys* are not conspicuously different from many species of *Rana*. In fact for many years they were treated as members of that genus. However, they have remarkably distinctive tadpoles, providing the main reason for regarding them as a separate group. These frogs are inhabitants of primary or secondary forests but only in hilly or mountainous country with clear, rocky streams where there are suitable breeding sites. Juveniles and adults often wander through the forest far from the streams where adults breed and tadpoles develop. Calling males perch on rocks or low vegetation on stream banks, and although many males may be calling on

117

a given night, they do not clump together. Eggs are laid near rapids and the hatching tadpoles quickly move into the swift water where they complete their development. Adults feed on medium-sized to large insects and other invertebrates, including such noxious animals as centipedes and scorpions. Tadpoles feed on a thin film of algae that grows on rocks in swift water of clear streams, relying on heavy beaks to scrape off the algae while clinging to the rocks by means of an abdominal sucker (see below).

Description—adults: *Meristogenys* are small (males of some species) to large frogs (females of some species), with moderately slender bodies and very long, slender legs. The snout in most species is narrow, but rounded. The eye is large and the eardrum is visible. The tips of fingers and toes are expanded into slightly pointed pads that are only about half as wide as the eardrum. The toes are fully webbed except for the pads. The skin is usually finely pebbled or smooth with a low, narrow ridge or fold of skin on each side of the back. In most species the back and top of head are medium to dark brown, the sides are lighter, and the underside is white, sometimes with a yellow or lime-coloured tint. The eye in some species is golden green in the upper half and golden brown in the lower, or with a narrow strip of dark red separating the two.

Adult males have a small, thin-skinned pouch at each side of the throat near the angle of the jaws. When they call, the vocal sacs puff out into these pouches. In most species the eardrum is conspicuously larger in males than in females.
Males: 34–68 mm.
Females: 57–93 mm.

The calls that are known are mostly high-pitched, single squeaks or chirps.

Tadpoles: The tadpoles of this genus are specialized for a life in strong currents, with a heavy body that is broadly rounded at the snout and flat below. The large mouth is on the underside of the snout and is followed by a large abdominal sucker that covers the abdomen. The mouth has heavy black, ribbed beaks. The upper beak is M-shaped, with a narrow gap in the centre dividing it into two pieces. The lower beak is V-shaped and may or may not be divided in the centre. The tail is about one and one-half times the length of the body, and has a very heavy muscle but low fins. These tadpoles also have small poison glands in clusters on the body and the tail fins, but the arrangement differs among species.

The tadpole of *Huia cavitympanum* has the same general form as *Meristogenys* tadpoles and a large sucker. But the mouth of *Huia* tadpoles differ in the number of rows of fine teeth and in the structure of the beak, details not easily visible to anyone without a microscope.

In most groups of frogs the tadpoles of related species are more difficult to separate than the adults. But in *Meristogenys* the reverse is true. Adults of *Meristogenys* do not differ greatly in form or colour. For this reason we are presenting descriptions of only three species, which represent the major types of variation among adults in the genus. Our notes on adults of *M. phaeomerus* would apply with very little change to adults of *M. amoropalamus*, *M. jerboa*, *M. macrophthalmus*, *M. orphnocnemis*, and *M. poecilus*. None of these species is distributed throughout Borneo, but one or several species occur in all hilly and mountainous parts of Borneo.

Meristogenys kinabaluensis (Inger)
Montane Torrent Frog (Fig. 61)

Description: A medium-sized to large frog with long legs. The triangular head is about as wide as the body. All toes are fully webbed. The back and top of the head are reddish brown mixed with olive green, or mostly olive green with brown spots. The sides of the head and body are bright olive green, becoming yellow towards the belly. There is a dark streak running between the eye and the nostril. The limbs are brown with dark crossbars. The underside of the head and body are silvery or yellowish white, sometimes with brown spots or markings on the throat.
Males: 58–68 mm.
Females: 75–93 mm.

Tadpole: This is a typical *Meristogenys* tadpole, with a large abdominal sucker and a muscular tail. The lower beak is an uninterrupted V-shaped structure. There are no poison glands in the tail fins. The body is mostly brown or black on the upper surfaces. Total length reaches 55–60 mm.

R.F. Inger

Fig. 61. *Meristogenys kinabaluensis* (Inger).

Habits and habitat: These frogs live along rocky banks of mountain streams of submontane forests from 650 to 2000 metres above sea level. The tadpoles cling to rocks in swift flowing currents.

Call: Unknown.

Distribution: Known only from the mountains of western Sabah and northern Sarawak.

Meristogenys phaeomerus (Inger & Gritis)
Brown Torrent Frog (Fig. 62)

Description: A medium-sized frog with long, slender legs and a triangular head. The eye is large. All the toes are fully webbed, except for the fourth (the longest), which usually has one joint free of webbing. The upper surfaces are medium to dark brown, often with small darker spots on the back. There is usually a narrow black border on the side just below the back. The upper surfaces of the limbs have dark crossbars. The undersides are white, but in some frogs the rear of the belly and the underside of the legs are lime-yellow or lemon-yellow. Males have distinctly larger eardrums than the females.

Males: 34–43 mm.

Females: 57–72 mm.

R.F. Inger

Fig. 62. *Meristogenys phaeomerus* (Inger & Gritis).

Tadpole: A typical *Meristogenys* tadpole with a large abdominal sucker on the flattened underside. Both beaks have a narrow gap in the centre. There are no poison glands on the tail fins. These tadpoles are unique within the genus in having a yellowish green body marked with black spots. Total lengths reach 30–35 mm.

Habits and habitat: This frog is common in hilly lowland forest, either primary or old secondary. Adults are sometimes found far from streams, but usually they stay close to the banks of medium-sized, clear, rocky streams. Almost every night a few calling males are scattered along the bank, with an occasional night in which they are present in large numbers. At no time do calling males form dense groups. Tadpoles cling to boulders and bedrock in rapids.

Call: A high-pitched squeak.

Distribution: Known from Kalimantan and southern and western Sarawak.

Meristogenys whiteheadi (Boulenger)
Whitehead's Torrent Frog (Fig. 63)

Description: A medium-sized to large species with very long hind limbs. All toes are fully webbed. The back and top of the head are dark brown. There is usually a dark streak on the side of the head from the eye to the nostril. The sides are lighter than the back and usually spotted with dark brown. The upper surfaces of the legs are dark brown with narrow lighter crossbars. The chest and belly are white and the throat mottled with brown. The top half of the eye is bright yellowish green. The eardrum of males is not noticably larger than that of females.
Males: 50–64 mm.
Females: 75–91 mm.

Fig. 63. *Meristogenys whiteheadi* (Boulenger).

Tadpole: A large abdominal sucker covers the underside of the body. The lower beak is V-shaped and undivided. Tadpoles have small poison glands that appear as small black spots in the lower fin where it meets the tail muscle. This is the largest tadpole in the genus with total lengths reaching 65–77 mm.

Habits and habitat: This species lives in primary and old secondary forest in mountainous country below 750 metres. Adults have been found only on the banks of streams where they perch on large rocks and low vegetation. Tadpoles live in torrents.

Call: Unknown.

Distribution: Known only from the mountainous parts of western Sabah and northern Sarawak.

Genus *Occidozyga*
Seep and Puddle Frogs

These small frogs live on the floor of lowland forest usually in seepage areas, small pools, or marshy ground. Both species are well camouflaged, *O. baluensis* to wet patches of soil and gravel and *O. laevis* to muddy water. Although they have stout, muscular legs, they usually make only short hops. The tadpoles are unusual both in form (see below) and habits. Instead of scraping at the bottom mud of streams or ponds and feeding on decaying plant fragments and algae, the tadpoles of *Occidozyga* rest on the bottom and prey on small insects or their larvae, which they probably capture by making short lunges.

Description—adults: Small, stocky frogs, with short hind limbs. Skin hides the eardrum. The snout is flattened, making the eyes seem more prominent. The tips of the toes are slightly expanded into small, rounded pads.

Tadpoles: The bodies and tails are very slender, with very low tail fins. The mouth is at the end of the snout, instead of just under the tip as in

123

most tadpoles. The lips lack the rows of fine black teeth that characterize the lips in other tadpoles of this family.

Occidozyga baluensis (Boulenger)
Seep Frog (Fig. 64)

Description: A small, stocky frog with a moderately pointed snout and short, stocky hind limbs. The toes are about three-quarters webbed. The skin of the back is smooth or faintly wrinkled, usually with a short ridge at the nape behind the eye. The middle of the back has a weak U-shaped ridge open to the rear.

Colouration is variable. In most individuals the top of the head and front of the back are tan or clay-coloured and the rear of the back dark brown or purplish black. The upper surfaces of the limbs are tan with dark crossbars. The underside is cream, heavily spotted with brown.
Males: 15–25 mm.
Females: 25–35 mm.

Tadpole: Tail more than twice the body length. Colour pale tan with a black streak from the lower front corner of the eye to the snout and a dark

R.F. Inger

Fig. 64. *Occidozyga baluensis* (Boulenger).

vertical bar below the eye. The tail muscle and narrow upper fin have small dark spots. Total length reaches 26 mm. See also under genus.

Habits and habitat: This small forest frog is almost always found where water seeps from a slope into a small flattish area. Its blotched colour pattern makes for remarkable camouflage in these patches of reddish clay and tan or brown pebbles. Unless it hops, it is almost invisible. The adults feed on small insects and other invertebrates, such as small spiders. The tadpoles live in the same seepage areas and are often in only a thin film of water, leaving their bodies mostly out of water.

Call: Unknown.

Distribution: Known from Kalimantan, Sabah, and Sarawak. It probably also occurs in Brunei.

Occidozyga laevis (Günther)
Yellow-Bellied Puddle Frog (Fig. 65)

Description: A small, squat, stocky frog with short, fat hind limbs. The toes are fully webbed and have round tips. This species is very similar in appearance to young *Rana kuhlii* except that in *O. laevis* the distance between the eyes is about the same or narrower than the width of the eyelid. Also the inside of the tip of the lower jaw is unlike that of *R. kuhlii* in having only a single tooth-like projection instead of a pair. The skin of the back and upper surfaces of the limbs has a uniformly corrugated appearance with occasional rounded bumps. The frogs are uniform dark gray-brown, though a few individuals have a wide light stripe down the middle of the back. The underside of the head is often speckled dark gray, and there is usually a lemon yellow tinge over the belly and underside of the thighs.
Males: 21–31 mm.
Females: 35–48 mm.

Tadpole: A small, very slender tadpole with a tail longer than twice the body length. The body and the margins of the fins have dark spots. Total length reaches 25 mm. See also under genus.

Habits and habitat: This forest species prefers marshy areas, muddy puddles, and very small streams and apparently does not live in groups. It is also found in and around rhino and pig wallows and even in water-filled elephant footprints. Frequently, adults sit or float almost submerged in water. In this position the colouration of the adult corresponds closely to the colour of turbid water. They feed on insects and will even eat small freshwater prawns. Most tadpoles have been found in shallow marshes. This species has been found only at low elevations.

Call: Unknown.

Distribution: Known from Kalimantan, Sabah, and Sarawak. Although *O. laevis* has been recorded from Peninsular Malaysia, Sumatra, Java, and the Philippine Islands, it is not certain that all of these frogs are members of the same species.

Fig. 65. *Occidozyga laevis* (Günther).

126

Genus *Rana*

This is one of the largest genera, in terms of numbers of species, in the Bornean fauna. Because the species of *Rana* are so heterogeneous in general form and habits, herpetologists have been arguing for years about dividing the genus into several genera, but have not reached any agreement. In this book we will use the name *Rana* the way we did in the first edition in order to avoid confusion.

As implied above, the Bornean species of this genus have very diverse habits and form. They range in size from small to very large. Some live along the banks of medium-sized to large rivers, some live in swamps, some live on forest floors, and some live in rice fields. Some remain at ground level and some climb into shrubs and trees. The tadpoles of some species develop in small to large streams, others develop in isolated rain pools on the floor of forests, and still others develop in flooded rice fields and ditches. Because of this great diversity, we do not present generalized descriptions as we have for other genera.

Rana baramica Boettger
Brown Marsh Frog (Fig. 66)

Description: A small to medium-sized frog with a rather wide head and a large prominent eye. The eardrum is visible. The toes are less than half-webbed. The fingers are long and the tips are slightly enlarged. The skin of the back and sides have scattered, small, rounded bumps. This species is dark brown above with indistinctinct, narrow, lighter areas. The sides are yellowish marked with irregular dark brown spots. The lips are marked with black bars separated by small white spots. The lower surfaces are whitish, with irregular brown or black markings.
Males: 38–46 mm.
Females: 44–67 mm.

Rana baramica is very similar to *R. glandulosa*, but is smaller; the males of *R. glandulosa* are as large or larger than females of *R. baramica*. Also the warts or lumps of skin on the sides of *R. glandulosa* are much larger than those of *R. baramica*.

C.L. Chan

Fig. 66 (above). *Rana baramica* Boettger. **Fig. 67** (below). *Rana cancrivora* Gravenhorst.

R.B. Stuebing

Tadpole: Tadpoles of this species have not yet been found in Borneo.

Habits and habitat: *Rana baramica* has been found in Borneo mostly in swamp forests near the coast. Adults live on the forest floor, but also climb up into low vegetation. Like the related species *R. glandulosa*, males call singly.

Call: A repetitive low chirp.

Distribution: Lowland coastal forests of Brunei, Kalimantan, Sabah, and Sarawak.

Rana cancrivora Gravenhorst
Mangrove Frog (Fig. 67)

Description: A medium-sized frog with a long snout and well-muscled hind limbs. The toes are more than half-webbed with the ends of the toes free of webbing. The tips of the toes are not swollen. The eardrum is conspicuous. The back and sides have short ridges and round bumps. The frogs are brown to bray on the back and legs, with dark markings. There is a dark bar across the top of the head between the eyes, and four to five dark bars across the top of the legs. The underside of the head varies from white to whiat with dark mottling. Males have a dark area under the corner of the jaw in the skin overlying the vocal sacs. Some individuals have dark spots on the chest and belly, where others are creamy white.
Males: 51–70 mm.
Females: 53–82 mm.

Tadpole: The tadpole has an oval body and is dark gray with darker spots. The tail is less than twice the body length.

Habits and habitat: This is a frog of disturbed habitats near the coast and mangrove. It is the only Malaysian frog that tolerates saline habitats. Although in Peninsular Malaysia it occurs in coastal rice fields, it is not known from such places in Borneo. Males do not form calling groups, but call singly from river banks, ditches, and other coastal waterways. The diet consists of a variety of small invertebrates, including crabs.

Distribution: Kalimantan, Sabah, and Sarawak. Also known from southern Thailand to Java and the Philippine Islands.

Rana chalconota (Schlegel)
White-Lipped Frog (Fig. 68)

Description: A small to memdium-sized frog with a distinctly pointed head and clearly visible eardrum. The legs are moderately long, and the toes are fully webbed, except perhaps the longest (fourth). The tips of all toes and fingers are distinctly expanded, forming rounded disks. The skin of the back is finely pebbled with an indistinct ridge or fold along each side. The back is a rich green by day and brown at night. The sides of the head and body are usually brown or olive. The upper lip is pearly white, at least from below the eye to the rear of the mouth. The underside of the head is mottled brown, with more scattered brownish spots down a whitish chest and belly. The underside of the legs is usually reddish.
Males: 33–44 mm.
Females: 46–59 mm.

R.F. Inger

Fig. 68. *Rana chalconota* (Schlegel).

Tadpole: The tadpole of this species is one of the few conspicuously marked tadpoles in Borneo. The body is pale yellow or straw-coloured, with black bars or spots below, in front, and behind the eye. On the underside of the oval, slightly flattened body, there are many small white glands arranged in two long patches, one on each side of the belly.

Habits and habitat: This species wanders freely through primary and disturbed forests and may even occur in wooded gardens. The usual perching site is in shrubs and small trees. Males form large calling groups at frequent intervals at side pools of medium-sized streams and at the edges of ponds. Adults feed on many kinds of insects and spiders.

Tadpoles live in quiet water, mostly in shallow side pools of streams where they grub in the debris of dead leaves that line the bottom.

Call: A staccato series of clicking notes.

Distribution: Common in all parts of lowland Borneo. Also found from southern Thailand to Java.

Rana erythraea (Schlegel)
Green Paddy Frog (Fig. 69)

Description: A small to medium-sized frog with long, muscular hind limbs and a long tapered snout. The toes are about half webbed, with the longest toe (the fourth) free of webbing near the tip. The tips of the toes and fingers are expanded slightly and round. The eardrum is prominent. The skin is smooth, though there is a low, wide ridge on each side of the back. This species is bright to dark green on the top of the head, down the back, and along the sides. There is a wide yellow stripe from behind the eye to the end of the body on each side. The upper lip is white and joins a white stripe running over the arm pit and along the lower part of the side. The upper surfaces of the limbs are light brown with fine dark markings. The underside is pearly white, occasionally with slight dark mottling towards the outer edges.
Males: 32–45 mm.
Females: 48–75 mm.

Fig. 69. *Rana erythraea* (Schlegel).

Tadpole: the body is oval and the tail rather deep and tapering near the end to a narrow tip. The body and tail are green or brown with dark speckling.

Habits and habitat: This is a frog of disturbed freshwater habitats such as irrigation ditches and, especially, flooded rice fields. They are extremely wary and it is difficult to get close to them even at night. Males do not form calling groups, but may be localized within a small area. They usually perch on grass or reeds, while females are more often seen on banks. *Rana erythraea* eats small terrestrial invertebrates, such as small millipedes, crickets, and ants. The tadpoles live in standing water.

Call: A squeaky warble.

Distribution: Brunei, Kalimantan, Sabah, and Sarawak. This species is widely distributed in Southeast Asia.

Rana finchi Inger
Rough Guardian Frog (Figs. 12, 13 & 70)

Description: A small, moderately stocky frog with relatively long hind limbs and thick thighs. The toes are partially webbed, and the ends of the toes slightly swollen. The eardrum is visible. The back has a distinct inverted V-shaped ridge in the middle and a series of interrupted short ridges along the sides. The upper eyelids have a number of small bumps. The frogs are brown to dark brown, with dark markings, including a dark bar across the top of the head between the eyes. The chin and throat are are darkly mottled, while the chest, belly, and underside of the thigh are either white or have a yellowish tinge.
Males: 32–39 mm.
Females: 39–45 mm.

Tadpole: The tadpole of this species has a slender, oval body and a tail shaped like a slender leaf. The mouth, just below the tip of the snout, is narrow. The body has irregular dark spots, and the tail has vertical dark bars. When nearing metamorphosis the tadpole is about 25 mm.

Fig. 70. *Rana finchi* Inger.

Habits and habitat: This frog lives on the floor of primary and old secondary forests at low elevations. It does not occur in swamp forests. Males call singly from under dead leaves at night. A female lays it eggs next to the male, who remains with the eggs. Usually the eggs are stuck to the underside of the leaf sheltering the male. When the tadpoles hatch, they somehow attach themselves to the back of the male who then carries them to a rain pool or a small intermittent stream where the tadpoles swim off to complete their development. Adults feed on small insects and spiders.

Call: A short trill.

Distribution: Known only from Sabah, though it may occur in eastern parts of Kalimantan.

Rana glandulosa Boulenger
Rough-Sided Frog (Fig. 71)

Description: A medium-sized frog with a broad head and prominent eyes. The toes are only half webbed, and have thickened, triangular pads at their tips. The fingers are long and have pads at the tips like hose of the toes. The eardrum is large. The skin is covered with slightly raised, round bumps that are most prominent along the sides of the body and the tops of the legs. There is a short ridge of skin running back from the upper eyelid and ending above the eardrum. These frogs are brown to dark brown with dark spots on the back. The sides are lighter brown and have large dark blotches. The chin, throat, chest, and belly are whitish with many brown spots. The under surface of the legs are white tinged with brown.
Males: 58–93 mm.
Females: 65–84 mm.

Tadpole: Tadpoles have not yet been found in Borneo. Those from West Malaysia have oval bodies and a tail that is twice the length of the body and pointed at the tip. The body and tail are reddish brown and spotted with dark brown. Mature tadpoles are about 55 mm long.

R.B. Stuebing

Fig. 71. *Rana glandulosa* Boulenger.

Habits and habitat: In Borneo this frog lives mainly in swampy forest and is more common along the coast. We have found it as high as 700 metres above sea level. The species lives on the forest floor. Little is known of its breeding behaviour but males call singly. Adults eat insects and other invertebrates.

Call: A loud resonant WAHK! in rapid sequence.

Distribution: Recorded from Brunei, Sabah, and Sarawak. It probably occurs in Kalimantan. Elsewhere reported from Peninsular Malaysia and Sumatra.

Rana hosii Boulenger
Poisonous Rock Frog. (Fig. 72)

Description: A medium (males) to large-sized (females) frog, with a moderately slender body and long, strong hind limbs. The tips of the fingers and toes are expanded into pads. The toes are fully webbed. The skin of the back is finely pebbled. A weak fold of sking is usually present on each side. The top of the head and the back are a rich, deep green. The sides are usually brown, and the upper surface of the legs light brown with dark crossbars. The belly is grayish or silvery white. Although not unusual, this is one of the most handsome frogs in Sabah.
Males: 45–68 mm.
Females: 86–100 mm.

Tadpole: The tadpoles of this species have not been described.

Habits and habitat: Adult *Rana hosii* are never found more than a few metres from the edge of rocky creeks or rivers. Although more common in primary forest, it also lives in partially logged forest provided a swift, clear stream is available. The frogs perch on rocks or shrubs and small trees overhanging streams, particularly where the current is strongest. If

R.B. Stuebing

Fig. 72. *Rana hosii* Boulenger.

disturbed while sitting on a rock, one of these frogs can skip across the surface of water to another rock. Males form loose calling groups.

Although the skin secretions of this species can kill small animals, such as other frogs, it is not dangerous for people unless one absent-mindedly rubs one's eyes after handling a frog. Always wash the hands thoroughly after handling this species.

Call: A weak chirp.

Distribution: Found throughout Borneo in appropriate environments from near sea level to about 750 metres. It also occurs in Peninsular Malaysia and Sumatra.

Rana ibanorum Inger
Rough-Backed River Frog (Fig. 73)

Description: A large, robust frog with a long and relatively pointed snout. The fingers are rounded and blunt,with no webbing, although there are narrow flaps of skin along both edges of the second and third fingers. The toes are blunt and fully webbed. The eardrum is visible. A series of short, mostly parallel ridges cover most of the back and the skin between them has low radiating lines. Adults are mostly grayish brown to blackish brown, and the throat is whitish with dark blotches. The rest of the lower surface is pure white.
Males: 80–130 mm.
Females: 80–101 mm.

Tadpole: The body is oval and relatively slender. The tail is slender and about twice the length of the body. The body is grayish brown with darker mottling which extends on to the tail. Mature tadpoles are about 35 mm long.

Habits and habitat: This species is common along clear, rocky streams 10 to 30 metres wide in primary and old secondary growth forests in hilly country. Adults are never found more than a few metres from stream banks. They feed on large insects, but also take crabs, small

Fig. 73. *Rana ibanorum* Inger.

lizards, and probably frogs. The tadpoles live in quiet side pools of these rocky streams and feed on organic debris, such as decaying leaves.

Call: Males do not have vocal sacs and have never been heard to call.

Distribution: Brunei, Sarawak, and Kalimantan. The species does not occur in Sabah and has never been found outside of Borneo.

Rana ingeri Kiew
Greater Swamp Frog (Fig. 74)

Description: This is a large heavy-bodied frog, with heavily muscled legs. It is similar to *Rana leporina*, except that the top and side of the snout do not form a sharp angle as in *R. leporina*, but are rounded. The eardrum is very distinct. The toes are fully webbed and have slightly swollen tips. The back has a few short ridges and the sides have a few scattered bumps. The upper eyelid is rough. The upper surfaces are reddish brown to dark brown, with indistinct darker markings. Unlike *R. leporina*, this species has no dark strips from the eye to the nostril. The chin and throat are heavily mottled with gray-brown. The chest and belly are grayish white with indistinct mottling.

138

Males: 75–132 mm.
Females: 70–127 mm.

Tadpole: The tadpole of this species looks very similar to those of *R. leporina* and *R. ibanorum*. It is oval, slender, and with a tail about twice the length of the body. The body is irregularly spotted and the tail is speckled with dark brown or black.

Habits and habitat: This species lives in both primary and disturbed forests, and may even be found in rubber plantations. It is often encountered in swampy areas and along muddy streams. Adults of this species are always found singly. Tadpoles live in quiet side pools of streams. Adults feed on large prey, including crabs, frogs, and even small snakes.

Call: Males have no vocal sacs and are not known to call.

Distribution: Brunei, Sabah, and Sarawak, not known outside of Borneo.

Fig. 74. *Rana ingeri* Kiew.

Rana kuhlii Dumeril & Bibron
Kuhl's Creek Frog (Fig. 75)

Description: A short stocky frog, with heavy legs. Adult males have a grotesquely broad head. The eardrum is not visible. The toes are fully webbed to the slightly swollen tips. In males the front of the lower jaw has a pair of large toothlike projections which are visible only when the mouth is opened. The skin of the back and sides has many small, rounded bumps. Frogs from most parts of Borneo have the hind limbs covered with very rough warts each of which has a small whitish cone at the centre. In parts of Sarawak the frogs have relatively smooth legs. The upper surfaces are dark gray to black with indistinct black blotches. The chin and throat are heavily spotted, while the rest of the underside is usually white. The underside of the legs may be darkly spotted.
Males: 44–74 mm.
Females: 51–67 mm.

Tadpole: Generally similar to tadpole of *R. leporina*, with an oval body and tail slightly less than twice the length of the body. The body is grayish brown with a narrow dark band acroos the body just behind the eyes and a second band at the end of the body. The tail has strong black vertical bands. When fully grown the tadpoles are 25–30 mm.

Habits and habitat: This frog lives in primary or old secondary forests in hilly country from near sea level to 1600 metres. It is almost never found more than a few metres from the banks of small to medium-sized streams (5–10 metres wide). It is common along such streams, but usually rare where the Giant River Frog (*R. leporina*) is abundant. Kuhl's Creek Frog clearly prefers rocky areas with moderate current and may be seen at night sitting on rocks within a few centimetres of the water. Adults do not form groups. Tadpoles are found in very small streams, or even in isolated pools of streams that have interrupted flow.

Call: Males do not have vocal sacs and those living at low elevations do not call. Males living at higher elevations on Mount Kinabalu emit a soft "TWEET."

Distribution: Known from all hilly parts of Borneo. The species also occurs through most of Southeast Asia.

140

Fig. 75. *Rana kuhlii* Dumeril & Bibron.

Rana laticeps Boulenger
Rivulet Frog (Fig. 76)

Description: A small stocky frog with heavy hind limbs and a wide head. It is very similar to Kuhl's Creek Frog in general shape and colour and in lacking a visible eardrum. But it is smaller and the toes are less than fully webbed. The skin of the back and sides is wrinkled and has scattered, small bumps. These frogs are brown or olive-brown with irregular black markings on the back. There is usually a dark streak between the eyes and red and black bars on the lips. The chest, belly, and underside of the legs are lemon yellow.
Males: 28–35 mm.
Females: 32–40 mm.

Tadpoles: Unknown, but probably very much like those of the related species *R. kuhlii*.

Fig. 76. *Rana laticeps* Boulenger.

Habits and habitat: This species has been found on the banks of small intermittent streams and in seepages near streams in primary forest at elevations below 500 metres. Little is known of its habits.

Call: Unknown.

Distribution: In Borneo known only from Sarawak. The species also occurs in Peninsular Malaysia and Thailand.

Rana leporina Andersson
Giant River Frog (Fig. 77)

Description: A large frog with a rather long tapered snout and large, powerful hind iimbs. The top and side of the snout meet at a sharp angle, and the eardrum is clearly visible. The toes are fully webbed and slightly swollen at the tips. The back has scattered short ridges and bumps that tend to disappear as the frog gets larger. The upper eyelid also has small bumps. The frogs are reddish brown to brown, with dark markings. There is always a dark streak on the side of the snout between the eye and the nostril. and often a dark W-shaped mark between the shoulders, particularly in young frogs. The underside is white with gray mottling on the chin and throat.

Males: 90–175 mm.

Females: 85–125 mm.

Tadpole: The tadpole has a slender, oval shape and a long tail. The mouth is just below the tip of the snout. The general colour is gray-brown, with dark markings, which form an almost zigzag row of dark spots on the tail. When ready to metamorphose, tadpoles of this species are about 36 mm long.

Habits and habitat: This is a frog of both primary and disturbed forests, from near sea level to about 750 metres. It lives along banks of large or medium-sized streams, either turbid or clear. Males have no vocal sacs and no "advertisement" call, and are usually widely spaced. The male however scoops out a shallow depression a a sand or gravel bar where the female lays her eggs. The tadpoles live in shallow side pools and in accumulations of dead leaves, which are a common feature of the the bottom of Bornean forest streams.

R.F. Inger

Fig. 77. *Rana leporina* Andersson.

Adults feed on a variety of large prey, including crabs and even other frogs.

Distribution: Found throughout Borneo, wherever suitable streams and forest occur.

Note: In the first edition of this book, this species was called *Rana blythii*. Taxonomic study in the last three years has shown that the Borneo frog is a separate species from *R. blythii* proper, which appears to be confined to Peninsular Malaysia and Thailand.

Rana limnocharis Boie
Grass Frog (Fig. 78)

Description: A small frog with a long narrow head and a slender, oval body. The toes are pointed, and less than half webbed. The fingers are also pointed. The eardrum is visible. The skin is finely pebbled, with a series of low, interrupted ridges runnin down the back, becoming a line of bumps both on the rump and the sides. There is a fold of skin from the rear of the eye over the eardrum. The frogs are rusty brown to brownish gray gray above, with darker blotches on the back. There is usually a U- or W-shaped marking across the shoulders. Most individuals also have a light streak down the middle of the back from the nose to the anus. The lips are conspicuously barred brown and white. The undersides of the females are completely white. Males have black, M-shaped band across the throat.
Males: 32–50 mm.
Females: 49–58 mm.

Tadpole: The tadpole has an oval body, which is about half the length of the tail. The body is olive green above and on the sides, speckled with black. The underside is white. The end of the tail is barred with black or is entirely black. Total length reaches 45 mm.

Habits and habitat: The frog is confined to disturbed habitats associated with the activities of man, including rice fields, roadsides, lawns and football fields. So it occurs in villages and towns, as well as in agricultural fields. It gathers in large groups around standing water and choruses are often heard well into the morning after a night of heavy rain. It eats a variety of insects, millipedes, and occasionally snails.

Call: A raspy chirp, rapidly repeated.

Distribution: Widely distributed in all parts of Borneo, wherever the forests have been removed. It occurs throughout tropical Asia.

Fig. 78. *Rana limnocharis* Boie.

Rana luctuosa (Peters)
Mahogany Frog (Fig. 79)

Description: A small to medium-sized frog, neither stocky nor slender, with a triangular head and rather short legs. The toes are less than half webbed and have rounded tips. The eardrum is distinct and almost as large as the eye. The skin is entirely smooth. The colouration is unlike that of any other frog in Borneo. The top of the head and back are rich chocolate or reddish bown without markings of any kind, while the sides

145

Fig. 79. *Rana luctuosa* (Peters).

Fig. 80. *Rana malesiana* Kiew.

of the head and trunk are black. A thin light line, from the tip of the snout to the end of the body, separates the brown and black surfaces. The fore and hind limbs have jet black bars separated by pale blue areas. The undersides are dark.

Males: 53–59 mm.

Females: 53–60 mm.

Tadpole: A robust, moderately large tadpole. The entire tadpole is dark gray or brown with irregular darker speckling over the body and tail. Total length reaches 65 mm.

Habits and habitat: Very little is known about this forest species. The only adult ever seen away from a breeding site was hiding under dead leaves on the forest floor. The species breeds at rain pools, where males form calling groups. Each male calls from a small hole it has excavated adjacent to the pool. Whether mating takes place in the hole and the pair then moves to the pool or the male emerges when a female approaches is unknown. The tadpoles develop in pools usually deeper than 30 cm, but some tadpoles have been found in shallow rhino wallows.

Call: A muted, meow-like note.

Distribution: Known so far from Sabah and Sarawak. Outside of Borneo it occurs in Peninsular Malaysia.

Rana malesiana Kiew
Peat Swamp Frog (Fig. 80)

Description: A large, stout frog with a broad head and thick, stocky limbs. The toes are about three-fourths webbed and are slightly swollen at the tips. The eardrum is visible. Males have long fang-like structures on the lower jaw as in Kuhl's Creek Frog. The skin is generally smooth, with some scattered low bumps on the back and sides. Most frogs are reddish brown, with fewer specimens a chocolate brown. Several wide black bars run from the eye across the lips. In most individuals, there is a fine, whitish line running from the tip of the snout, between the eyes and down the middle of the back. There is often a similar fine line on the upper surfaces of the legs. The throat and chest have dark mottling, and the underside of the hind limb is very dark.

Males: 70–150 mm.

Females: 75–95 mm.

Tadpole: Tadpoles are slim, oval, and have slender tails. The colour is golden brown mottled with dark pigment. Total length reaches 25 mm.

Habits and habitat: This frog is typical of peat swamps and low alluvial plains up to about 150 metres above sea level. It occurs both in primary and disturbed forests, such as old rubber plantations. Almost nothing is known of its breeding habits. The diet consists of a wide variety of invertebrates and small frogs.

Call: Unknown.

Distribution: Known from Kalimantan, Sabah, and Sarawak. Almost certainly it occurs in Brunei where much suitable habitat exists. The species also occurs in Peninsular Malaysia.

Rana nicobariensis (Stoliczka)
Cricket Frog (Fig. 81)

Description: A small to medium-sized frog with a long, narrow, pointed head. The eardrum is visible. The legs are slender, and the fingers and toes extremely long with slightly swollen tips. The toes are only about half webbed, and the longest toe extends far beyond the webbing. The skin of the back is finely pebbled, and there is a distinct thin ridge or fold of skin along each side. The back is brown, with dark spots. The entire upper lip is pearly white. The underside is dirty white with gray mottling.

Males: 37–47 mm.

Females: 47–53 mm.

Tadpole: Tadpoles have an oval body and a tail about twice the length of the body. The lower lip has long, finger-like projections. The body is light brown mottled with darker brown, and the tail has a dark network. Total length reaches 47 mm.

Habits and habitat: A widely distributed frog of disturbed habitats, found both along logging roads and streets in towns. The harsh call of the males is one of the characteristic sounds of wet grassy areas and roadside ditches. Males are often very abundant, but do not appear to call in groups. The species seems to breed year round. The tadpoles develop in the shallow water of ditches and temporary ponds. Adults will eat most kinds of insects of moderate size.

Call: Six to ten loud, sharp notes in rapid sequence.

Distribution: Reported from Kalimantan, Sabah, and Sarawak. It almost surely occurs in Brunei. The species is found from Thailand to Bali.

Fig. 81. *Rana nicobariensis* (Stoliczka).

149

Rana palavanensis Boulenger
Smooth Guardian Frog (Fig. 82)

Description: A small frog, with ong slender hind limbs. The toes are only about half-webbed and have slightly swoolen tips. The eardrum is visible. The skin of the back is smooth except for an inverted V-shaped ridge in the centre and a thin, continous ridge from the eye to the rump. The back is reddish to chocolate brown, with a dark bar across the top of the head between the eyes. The inverted V-shaped ridge is also edged in black. The underside of the head is grayish white, while the chest, belly, and undersides of the legs are usually lemon yellow.
Males: 25–30 mm.
Females: 35–40 mm.

Tadpole: The tadpoles are small, with the tail about twice the length of the body and tapering abruptly near the end to a narrow tip. The body is tan or dark brown and mottled with darker pigment. The tail is speckled with black. Total length reaches 30 mm.

Habits and habitat: This frog lives on the floor of primary forests from near sea level to 1300 metres. Its habits are very similar to those of *R. finchi*. Males are solitary, calling from under dead leaves. Eggs are laid in a manner similar to that of *R. finchi*, and the male carries the immature tadpoles on his back to small rain pools or isolated pools in small stream beds. The tadpoles complete their development in these small bodies of water. Adults prey on ants, termites, and other small invertebrates of the forest floor.

Call: A short, high-pitched trill.

Distribution: Kalimantan, Sabah, and Sarawak. It also occurs on Palawan Island in the Philippines.

Rana paramacrodon Inger
Lesser Swamp Frog (Fig. 83)

Description: A medium to stocky frog, with moderately long and muscled hind limbs. The snout ends in a rounded point. The eardrum is

150

R.B. Stuebing

Fig. 82. *Rana palavanensis* Boulenger.

R.F. Inger

Fig. 83. *Rana paramacrodon* Inger.

distinct. The tips of the toes are distinctly, but slightly widened; the tips of the fingers are not. All of the toes except the fourth (the longest) are webbed almost to the tips. The upper surfaces are roughly pebbled and there are a few low bumps on the back. The head and body are grayish to reddish brown above and on the sides. Most individuals have a dark streak on the side of the snout from the eye to the nostril. The distinctive feature of the colouration is a dark brown, almost black, diamond-shaped, mask-like spot that begins at the rear of the eye and covers the entire eardrum. The rear half of the belly and the underside of the legs are usually yellow.

Males: 60–75 mm.
Females: 55–66 mm.

Tadpole: Unknown.

Habits and habitat: This species has been found along clay and gravel banks of small streams in primary and selectiely logged rain forests at low elevations. It also occurs in peat swamps near the coast. Presumably, it breeds in such places as some of the females caught were gravid. Adults prey on a variety of insects and invertebrates of moderate to large size. One stomach contained a centipede 75 mm long.

Call: Unknown, but since males lack vocal sacs the species probably lacks an advertisement call.

Distribution: Known from Brunei, Kalimantan, Sabah, and Sarawak. It has also been found in Peninsular Malaysia and Singapore Island.

Rana picturata Boulenger
Spotted Stream Frog (Fig. 84)

Rana signata (Günther)
Striped Stream Frog (Fig. 85)

We group these species because they are so similar in habits and form, except for details of colouration (see accompanying photographs).

Description: Small to medium-sized frogs with a triangular head about same width as body. The eardrum is visible. Both fingers and toes have

R.B. Stuebing

Fig. 84 (above). *Rana picturata* Boulenger. **Fig. 85** (below). *Rana signata* (Günther).

R.F. Inger

slightly swollen tips and the toes are slightly more than half webbed. the skin of the back is very finely pebbled and the upper surfaces of the legs are almost smooth.

Both species are generally dark brown or black with lighter markings. The underside is dark gray with small lighter markings. Both species have red or orange markings on the upper surfaces of head and body. A common feature is a light orange or red stripe from the tip of the snout to to and along the edge of the upper eyelid.

In the striped stream frog (*R. signata*) the stripe on the edge of the eyelid is continued to the end of the body without interruption where the side meets the back. There may be a few light spots of the same colour in the centre of the back.

In the spotted stream frog (*R. picturata*) the stripe on the eyelid may not appear on the side of the back, but if it is present it is always interrupted. The centre area of the back is always marked with a number of irregular orange or red spots.
Males: 33–47 mm.
Females: 49–68 mm.

Tadpole: The tadpoles of both species have relatively slender bodies and tails and are almost black. Small glands that appear as fine light dots are scattered over the tail fins and are grouped in small patches under the body. Total lengths reach 41 mm.

Larvae of the two species differ in the arrangement and number of glands under the body, but these features cannot be seen without the aid of a good microscope.

Habits and habitat: These frogs live along banks of small to medium-sized streams in primary or slightly disturbed forests at elevations from near sea level to about 750 metres. Males call from irregularities in the banks of streams or from small roots that project from the banks. Almost every night a few solitary males can be heard, while at odd intervals a large calling aggregation will form. Tadpoles live in shallow side pools or in accumulations of dead leaves that form in the bottoms of these streams. When they transform into froglets, they leave the stream and live in the forest leaf litter. They return to the stream as they approach adult size.

Call: The call of *R. picturata* consists of four to six grating notes, of sharply decreasing intensity. The call of *R. signata* has not been recorded.

Distribution: *Rana picturata* is found throughout Borneo. *Rana signata* is known primarily from coastal areas of Sarawak and western Sabah.

Genus *Staurois*

The species of this genus are streamside frogs, rarely found more than a few metres from clear water. They are common in the sense that they are widespread in areas of the appropriate environment, two of them (*S. latopalmatus* and *S. natator*) below 1000 metres and one (*S. tuberilinguis*) from about 400 to 1800 metres. They differ from one another in the kinds of perches they use. *Staurois latopalmatus* sits on rocks next to the strongest currents in rocky rivers, *S. natator* perches on twigs of shrubs overhanging sandy or rocky streams, and *S. tuberilinguis* is usually seen perched on stems and leaves of small herbs or ferns growing on rocks in midstream. Despite their wide distribution in Borneo, little is known of their tadpoles. The one type of tadpole known, that of *S. natator*, has been found in masses of dead leaves in pools within clear streams. The association of these species with clear water is so strong that all the hundreds of specimens recorded have come from hilly country; none have come from flat or flood plain forests, which invariably have turbid, silty streams.

Description—adults: Small to medium-sized frogs with long hind limbs. The tips of the fingers and toes are expanded into wide pads having a blunt end. The pads are oval rather than round. All toes are fully webbed to the pads. The eardrum is visible. The skin of the back is coarsely granular or set with round and oval swellings. Two species are narrow-bodied and long-nosed, while the third is squat and pug-nosed.

Staurois latopalmatus (Boulenger)
Rock Skipper (Fig. 86)

Description: This is a medium-sized species, with a body that is neither stocky nor slender. The snout is very short, rounded, and slopes back from its upper surface to the mouth. The legs are long and very heavily muscled. The two outer fingers are about half webbed. The entire upper

Fig. 86. *Staurois latopalmatus* (Boulenger).

surface has coarsely granular skin, while the belly is smooth. All upper surfaces are black with short, narrow yellowish or whitish markings. The underside is white or pale cream.
Males: 40–50 mm.
Females: 60–70 mm.

Tadpole: Unknown.

Habits and habitat: This species is found only on clear, swift, rocky streams. It perches on rocks, especially those with a vertical face, either on the bank or in mid-stream. If disturbed, it leaps from rock to rock or may even leap into swift water and skip across the surface to another rock. Although most frequently seen in primary forest, it can also live on streams flowing through logged areas if some trees remain and if the water is clear and the bottom free of silt.

Call: Unknown.

Distribution: Known from Kalimantan, Sabah, and Sarawak.

Staurois natator (Günther)
Black-Spotted Rock Frog (Fig. 87)

Description: A small frog with a pointed snout, narrow body, and long, slender hind limbs. The skin of the back is distinctly pebbled and set with small round, uniformly sized swellings. The belly is coarsely granular. The upper surfaces are olive green, with large black spots. The underside is bright yellowish green or lemon yellow. The upper surface of the three inner toes and the webbing between them is turquoise blue.

Fig. 87. *Staurois natator* (Günther).

157

Males: 29–37 mm.
Females: 44–55 mm.

Tadpole: The body is oval, a bit flattened, and less than half the tail length. The nostrils are just above the end of the snout. The eyes are small and in young tadpoles are covered with thick skin. The tail has very low fins and ends in a broad tip. The tadpoles are colourless, but the bellies appear pinkish because the circulating blood can be seen through the thin skin.

Habits and habitat: This is a frog of primary forest in hilly country, living along small rocky streams. Tadpoles have been found in accumulations of dead leaves in streams.

Call: A sharp chirp.

Distribution: Kalimantan, Sabah, and Sarawak. It is so widespread in those states that it must also occur in Brunei. It has also been found in the Philippine Islands.

Staurois tuberilinguis Boulenger
Green-Spotted Rock Frog (Fig. 88)

Description: A small, slender frog with a pointed snout and long, slender hind limbs. The skin of the back is finely pebbled with many round or oval, unequal-sized swellings. Some of the swellings may form an interrupted ridge from the eye to the base of the thigh. The upper surfaces are a slightly metallic hue of brown with irregular greenish patches. There is a greenish white patch behind the eye and a similarly coloured mottling along the side. The underside of the head is light blue-green, with dark spots. The chest and belly are bluish white. The tops of the three inner toes and the upper surface of the webbing are chalky bluish white.
Males: 23–27 mm.
Females: 29–36 mm.

Tadpole: Unknown.

158

Fig. 88. *Staurois tuberilinguis* Boulenger.

Habits and habitat: This is a frog of primary forest in hilly country from about 200 to 1800 metres above sea level, it is most common above 500 metres. It is never found away from small rocky streams. One frequently sees small mixed groups of juveniles and adults all clinging to one small stem or frond growing on rock in mid-stream.

Call: A thin metallic squeak.

Distribution: So far known only from Sabah and Sarawak.

CHAPTER 11

FAMILY RHACOPHORIDAE

T his is almost an exclusively Asian family, with only a few genera living in Africa and Madagascar. Almost all the species live above ground in bushes or trees. Most of them breed in standing water. A few Bornean species do not have free-swimming tadpoles.

Nyctixalus pictus (Peters)
Cinnamon Frog (Fig. 89)

Description: A small frog with a relatively long snout and long hind limbs. The eardrum is visible and a bit smaller than the diameter of the eye. The tips of the fingers and toes are expanded into round pads that are smaller than the eardrum. The toes are about half-webbed and the fingers lack webbing. The skin of the back, head, and the upper surfaces of the limbs is rough, with many small spiny bumps. All the upper surfaces and the sides tend to be cinnamon brown, though some individuals are red or even orange. Scattered over all are small glossy white spots that form a broken line from the edge of the snout, along the edge of the upper eyelid, and continuing part way down the side of the back. The upper half of the iris of the eye is also white; the lower half is brown. This is one of the most distinctly coloured of Bornean frogs; it cannot be mistaken for any other species.
Males: 30–33 mm.
Females: 31–34 mm.

Tadpole: The body is oval, almost as wide as long, and slightly flattened. The tail is less than twice the length of the body and tapers to a rounded tip. The body and tail muscle are purplish brown and the tail fins slightly lighter. Total lengths reach 44–53 mm.

Habits and habitat: This species lives in primary and old secondary

Fig. 89. *Nyctixalus pictus* (Peters).

forests, in flat and hilly terrain, and from near sea level to 1650 metres. It seems to be abundant and widespread in Borneo, as we have seen almost every place we have worked. Adults have been found on leaves of shrubs and small trees one to three metres above ground, but presumably reach higher levels. Two to four males may gather around water containing tree holes or cavities in logs. Tadpoles develop in such cavities, and once we found tadpoles in a rotting hollow fruit that contained water.

Call: Unknown.

Distribution: Recorded from all parts of Borneo except Brunei, where it probably occurs. This species also lives in Sumatra and Peninsular Malaysia.

Genus *Philautus*
Bush Frogs

These small frogs are among the most difficult for experts to identify. A few of the Bornean species are relatively easy to separate from the others, but most are troublesome even with a microscope. One distinctive characteristic of these frogs is that they lack a free-swimming tadpole. Females lay a few (less than 20) very large eggs and the embryo develops within the egg into a tiny froglet with a tail. Just before hatching the tail is absorbed just as in a "normal" tadpole.

Most species live scattered through primary forests, from near sea level to above 3000 metres on Mount Kinabalu. At night, males of most species call from leaves of shrubs one to three metres above the ground, often in small areas within a forest where it is unclear why the frogs would have chosen that particular site to call. A mated pair descends to the ground where the large eggs are deposited under dead leaves. Eggs of *Philautus* have also been found in pitcher plants, but it is not certain which species was the parent. One species, *Philautus hosii*, calls from vegetation on stream banks and appears to stick its eggs onto leaves overhanging water.

Because of the difficulties in identifying most of these species, we will give generalized descriptions that fit groups of them. Several features, however, are common to them all: the tips of the fingers and toes are expanded into round pads, and the toes are usually about half-webbed. As *Philautus* lacks free-swimming tadpoles, that part of the description is lacking in the following accounts.

Philautus aurantium Inger
Golden-Legged Bush Frog (Fig. 90)

Description: A very small, stocky frog with a wide head and moderately long legs. The eardrum is partly hidden by skin. The outer fingers have rather wide pads at their tips and a narrow web at their bases. The first toe has very little webbing, whereas the outer toes are a bit more than half-webbed. The upper surfaces are smooth, except for a curved fold of

R.F. Inger

Fig. 90. *Philautus aurantium* Inger.

R.F. Inger

Fig. 91. *Philautus bunitus* Inger, Stuebing & Tan.

skin from the eye to the arm pit. The underside of the body is coarsely pebbled.

The colour is pale sandy or pinkish brown. The back usually has black markings that curve from the centre towards each groin. The hidden surfaces of the thigh are golden yellow or orange.
Males: 24–28 mm.
Females: 26–27 mm.

Habits and habitat: This species lives in primary or selectively logged forest from 750 to 1040 metres above sea level. Males call from leaves of shrubs and trees between 0.5 and 3 metres above ground.

Call: Not described.

Distribution: So far known only from western Sabah.

Philautus bunitus Inger, Stuebing & Tan
Green Bush Frog (Fig. 91)

Description: A small, stocky frog with a wide head, a large eye, and a visible eardrum. The pads at the tips of the outer fingers are larger than the eardrum. The fingers have a narrow web at their base and usually a narrow fringe of skin. The toes are about three-fourths webbed. The head and back have small, scattered bumps, and the underside is coarsely pebbled. The head and back are leafy green with black speckling forming an indistinct pattern. The tops of the inner fingers and the webbing of the inner toes are yellow or orange. The belly and the underside of the inner fingers and toes are are orange or pale greenish orange.
Males: 35–41 mm.
Females: 44–46 mm.

Habits and habitat: This species lives in submontane and montane forests between 1350 and 1600 metres above sea level. Both males and females perch on leaves of shrubs and small trees from 0.5 to 4 metres above ground.

Call: Unknown.

Distribution: Known only from the mountains of western Sabah.

Philautus hosii (Boulenger)
Hose's Bush Frog (Fig. 92)

Description: A medium-sized frog with a sharp-edged snout. The eardrum is visible. The tips of the fingers are expanded into wide, round pads; the pad of the third finger is wider than the eardrum. Webbing on the fingers is limited to a narrow fringe at their base. The toes are almost fully webbed. The skin of the back is finely pebbled. There are two weak rows of small bumps forming an open V between the shoulders and several small bumps on the upper eyelid. There are no fleshy spines at the heel.

Fig. 92. *Philautus hosii* (Boulenger).

166

The colour is yellowish to dark sandy brown, usually with a dark triangle between the eyes and a thin dark X-shaped mark on the back. The sides have faint streaks of yellow. The upper third of the iris is pale gold and the lower portion light grayish brown.
Males: 40–49 mm.
Females: 51–63 mm.

Habits and habitat: This species lives in primary or old secondary forests, from near sea level to about 600 metres in both flat and hilly terrain. Most individuals have been found perched on leaves or twigs of shrubs and small trees 0.5–4 metres above the ground. Males call singly. We have found small groups of eggs adhering to leaves overhanging streams that we believe are those of this species.

Call: A staccato musical trill of five or six notes.

Distribution: Known from many places in Sarawak and Sabah.

Philautus ingeri Dring
Sharp-Snouted Bush Frog (Fig. 93)

Description: A small to medium-sized frog, with a pointed, sharp-edged snout. The eardrum is visible. The tips of the fingers are expanded into wide, round or oval pads. There is a narrow web at the base of the fingers and a thin fringe of skin running out the fingers to the pads. The fourth toe (the longest is half-webbed, but the third and fifth toes are almost fully webbed. The top of the head and back are finely pebbled. The upper eyelid has two or three small bumps and several others are scattered on the back. There are one or two short, fleshy spines at the heel.

The colour is pale sandy brown, lighter on the sides and with a sharp dark streak on the side of the snout between the eye and the nostril. There is usually a dark triangle between the eyes and sometimes a concave sided dark mark in the centre of the back. The upper third of the iris is pale gold and the lower two-thirds brown.
Males: 36 mm.
Females: 47–50 mm.

Habits and habitat: This species has been seen only in montane forests, from 1300 to 1500 metres above sea level. The frogs perch on shrubs 1–5 metres above the ground.

Call: A series of five soft notes.

Distribution: This species is known from the mountains of western Sabah and northeastern Sarawak.

Fig. 93. *Philautus ingeri* Dring.

Philautus petersi (Boulenger)
Brown Bush Frog (Fig. 94)

Description: A small, stout frog with a wide head. The snout is rounded in males, but in females it ends in a distinct, somewhat hardened cone. The eardrum is visible. The fingers have wide, rounded pads at the tips and narrow webbing at the base. Pads at the tips of the toes are a bit

168

smaller than those of the fingers. The toes are half to three-fourths webbed. The skin is finely pebbled on the upper surfaces with scattered bumps, especially on the eyelid, on the top of the snout, at the sides of the back, and upper surface of the limbs. Usually there is a soft, spine-like projection at the heel.

The colour is highly variable. The back and top of the head may be rich cinnamon brown with a black stripe curving along the back and side, or dark grayish brown with small black and yellowish spots, grayish brown on the head and fore part of the back and dark brown or black in the rear. The side of the head has dark bars radiating from the eye. The limbs have dark crossbars. The front and rear faces of the thigh are reddish.
Males: 21–24 mm.
Females: 29–34 mm.

Habits and habitat: This species lives in submontane and montane forests, from 1000 to 2000 metres above sea level. At night adults feed and call from shrubs between 0.5 and 3 metres above the ground. They hide under dead leaves during the day.

R.F. Inger

Fig. 94. *Philautus petersi* (Boulenger).

Call: A short high-pitched trill.

Distribution: Reported from Sarawak and western Sabah. It probably also occurs in mountainous areas of Kalimantan.

Note: With slight modifications, the description above could apply to *Philautus amoenus* (Sabah), *P. longicrus* (Sabah and Sarawak), *P. mjöbergi* (Sabah and Sarawak) (Fig. 95), *P. refugii* (Sarawak), and *P. umbra* (Sarawak). The last species is slightly larger than *P. petersi* and the second one slightly smaller. The females of most of these species do not have a cone on the tip of the snout.

Fig. 95 *Philautus mjöbergi* Smith.

Genus *Polypedates*

Three of the Bornean species of this genus live in primary or secondary forests in the lowlands. The exceptional species, *Polypedates leucomystax*, lives lives almost everywhere except primary forests—in towns, villages, agricultural fields, road sides, and cleared forests. Adults spend their time above ground in shrubs and trees, though how high they live in trees is not known. Again, *P. leucomystax* is an exception; it is often found at ground level, either in grass or under houses. All have

170

similar breeding habits. Males call around bodies of shallow standing water. The female when clasped by a male produces a foam nest, that is made by churning mucus with the hind limbs and is attached to leaves of shrubs overhanging water. The foam nest of *P. leucomystax* is often placed on the ground at water's edge. After hatching the tadpoles wriggle free of the nest and, if the foam mass has not already fallen on to the pool's surface, drop into the water.

Description—adults: Small to large frogs with a relatively slender, flattened body and long legs. The eardrum is visible. All have large round or oval pads at the tips of the fingers, which are long and lack webbing. The toes also have enlarged pads at the tips, but these are smaller than those of the fingers. The toes are almost fully webbed. The skin is smooth or finely pebbled on the upper surfaces. The belly is coarsely pebbled. Except for one species (*P. colletti*), the skin between the eyes is fused to the underlying skull.

Tadpoles: The tadpoles have fat, almost spheroidal bodies, with the eyes set at the sides of the head, enabling the tadpoles to see up or down. The tails have relatively high fins. The mouth is just below the tip of the snout and set with strong, black beaks.

Two features separate these species from the next genus, *Rhacophorus*. The adults of *Polypedates* have no webbing on the fingers, and the tadpoles of *Polypedates* have the eyes set at the side. All adults of *Rhacophorus* species have noticeable webbing on the hand and in all tadpoles the eyes are set on top of the head, not at the sides.

Polypedates colletti (Boulenger)
Collett's Tree Frog (Fig. 96)

Description: A small (males) to large (females) tree frog with a triangular head and distinctly pointed snout. The skin is smooth except for a fold over the eardrum. The skin on top of the head is not fused to the skull. These frogs are usually light tan or pinkish brown with a conspicuous dark mark on the back in the shape of an hour-glass or an X, though some individuals are unmarked. The sides have scattered dark spots and the limbs have dark crossbars.

Fig. 96. *Polypedates colletti* (Boulenger).

Males: 44–52 mm.
Females: 59–77 mm.

Tadpole: Although tadpoles assumed to be those *P. colletti* have been collected, their identification remains uncertain.

Habits and habitat: The species lives in primary and old secondary lowland and peat swamp forests, from near sea level to 650 metres. Adults descend from trees to breed around small pools of standing water.

Call: A series of harsh crackling notes.

Distribution: Recorded only from Sarawak and Sabah, probably more widespread.

Polypedates leucomystax (Gravenhorst)
Four-Lined Tree Frog (Fig. 97)

Description: A small to medium-sized frog with a slender body and long, slender hand limbs. The sides of the snout are sharp, but the tip is not. The skin is smooth except for a curved fold over the eardrum. These frogs vary from light beige to dark tan on the head, back, legs. Most individuals have four narrow dark stripes running down the back, while the rest have scattered brown spots.
Males: 37–50 mm.
Females: 57–75 mm.

C.L. Chan

Fig. 97. *Polypedates leucomystax* (Gravenhorst).

Tadpole: The body is slightly flattened above; the colour light buff or brown with irregular markings. Total lengths reach 50 mm. See also under genus.

Habits and habitat: This is a frog of disturbed habitats, found everywhere, including the inside of houses, but rarely entering primary forest. Males form calling groups around any standing water. We have even seen pairs mating at the edge of small, water-filled road ruts. Adults eat a variety of insects and other vertebrates.

Call: A low pitched nasal quack.

Distribution: Occurs throughout Borneo in disturbed environments as high as 750 metres above sea level. This species is widely distributed in southern Asia.

Polypedates macrotis (Boulenger)
Dark-Eared Tree Frog (Fig. 98)

Description: A medium-sized to large frog with a triangular head and large eyes. The skin is smooth, though some frogs have very small bumps on the back. Often there is a narrow, whitish ridge of skin along the outer edge of the forearm. This species is tan to brown on the head, back, and legs. Some individuals have a pair of wide black stripes down the back. There is a distinct dark brown band from the eye, covering the eardrum and becoming narrower as it continues along the side. The underside of the head is heavily mottled with brown.
Males: 45–57 mm.
Females: 66–85 mm.

Tadpole: Tadpoles have larger, deeper bodies and deeper tail fins than tadpoles of *P. leucomystax*. The body is dark green above speckled with lighter flecks, and the underside is silvery gray. Total lengths reach 55–60 mm. See also under genus.

Habits and habitat: This is a frog of primary and disturbed forests of the lowlands. It gathers in large groups in vegetation over standing water at forest edges. it may even breed at ditches surrounded by shrubs. Adults eat a wide variety of small insects and other invertebrates.

Call: A long drawn out chuckle, with the first note louder than the rest.

Distribution: Kalimantan, Sabah, and Sarawak. It almost certainly occurs in Brunei. The species has also been reported from Sumatra and the southern Philippine Islands.

W.M. Poon

Fig. 98. *Polypedates macrotis* (Boulenger).

Polypedates otilophus (Boulenger)
File-Eared Tree Frog (Fig. 99)

Description: A large tree frog, with a saw-edged bony ridge over the eardrum. The head is triangular with a protruding, sharp point at the angle of the jaw. The toes are only half-webbed. The skin is smooth, except for a pointed projection at the heel and a smaller one at the elbow.

175

Fig. 99. *Polypedates otilophus* (Boulenger).

The frogs are tan or yellowish with thin dark lines running down the back and head. The rear of the thigh is marked with eight to twelve bold black bars on a white background. The underside is a dirty white. This species has a distinctive, musty stench, which most people find offensive.

Males: 64–80 mm.

Females: 82–97 mm.

Tadpole: The tadpoles are very large (up to 60 mm long) and are yellowish green. The tail fins are quite deep. See also under genus.

Habits and habitat: This tree frog lives in both primary and disturbed forests, as well as in tree plantations. It has been found from near sea level to 1000 metres. Males call from vegetation around pools of standing water. Adults feed on a variety of insects, but especially on large tree crickets.

Call: A series of slurred, rasping notes followed by several loud "chucks."

Distribution: Known from Kalimantan, Sabah, and Sarawak. It also occurs on Sumatra.

Genus *Rhacophorus*

All the Bornean species of this genus of tree frogs live in forests, either primary or old secondary, most at low elevations though three are in montane environments. We do not know how high they climb above the forest floor, but we have seen tree frogs at least seven metres above the ground and have heard calls from individuals in the canopy. The Bornean species fall into several groups. First, there are those that breed in flowing water, including *R. angulirostris*, *R. bimaculatus*, and *R. gauni*, and are relatively small. All the other Bornean species breed in standing water, though two small species, *R. appendiculatus* and *R. kajau*, seem to use very shallow water, such as seeps and shallow swamps. The remainder are "pond" breeders, often using wallows made by forest pigs or rhinos. Also included in this genus are at least three

Bornean frogs that can glide; it is possible that more have this capacity. The known gliding species have extensively webbed fingers and toes, which greatly increase their surface area because they spread the fingers and toes immediately when they jump. It is likely that the gliding frogs use this ability to escape enemies and as a means of descending from the canopy of the forest to their breeding sites in low vegetation around ponds.

Description—adults: Small to large frogs with extensively webbed toes and at least some webbing between the fingers. There is some form of fringe or flaps or soft projections from the edge of the limbs and at the heel. All species have tips of fingers and toes expanded into wide, round or oval pads. The hind limbs are long and slender. The eardrum is visible. The eyes are large and the pupil contracts into a horizontal slit. Colouration varies widely, from bright green to orange to yellow to brown and from uniform to barred or mottled. The skin of the back is usually finely pebbled, but may have small bumps or projections.

Tadpoles: Most species have relatively large, fat tadpoles with relatively deep fins, but in some species they are small, slender, and have narrow tails. All usually have some markings.

Rhacophorus angulirostris Ahl
Masked Tree Frog (Fig. 100)

Description: A small frog with a wide head and a short pointed snout with sharp edges. The toes, except for the fourth, are webbed to the base of the pads. The two outer fingers are fully webbed to the pads. The skin is smooth on the head and back and granular on the chest and belly. The frogs are pale gray-green to sandy brown. Some individuals have dark crossbars on the back. The sides of the body and the inner surfaces of the legs are usually yellow with several large black spots. The chest and belly are pearly white.
Male: 31–33 mm.
Females: 45–51 mm.

Tadpole: The body is oval and slightly flattened above. The slender tail is twice as long as the body. The lips around the mouth are wide and

Fig. 100. *Rhacophorus angulirostris* Ahl.

form a cup-like structure. The body is dark, almost black on top and on the sides. The tail muscle has large dark spots and the upper fin has smaller ones. Total length reaches 36 mm.

Habits and habitat: This is a frog of primary forest, sporadically common along clear, rocky streams above 1000 metres. Calling males perch on small trees overhanging streams usually several metres above the water. The tadpoles live in gravel riffles.

Call: Not described.

Distribution: So far known only from the mountains of western Sabah.

Rhacophorus appendiculatus (Günther)
Frilled Tree Frog (Fig. 101)

Description: This small tree frog has a triangular head with an almost conical tip to the snout in males. In females the snout has an enlarged conical projection, giving them an odd "boat-nosed" appearance. The toes are about three-fourths webbed, with the ends of several toes projecting beyond the webbing. The two outer fingers are partially webbed, but the others are unwebbed. The skin of the upper surfaces is covered with many irregular small bumps, which tend to be larger on the sides. The outer edges of the forearm and the leg have a narrow wavy-edged fringe of skin. A narrow flap of skin skin runs across the body just below the vent. The upper surfaces are gray green to brown, with variable dark markings. The undersides of the head and body are whitish, with a very slight yellowish tinge. About half of the individuals have a pinkish tinge on the front of the thigh.

Males: 30–37 mm.

Females: 42–50 mm.

Tadpole: Body oval and rounded. The rather deep tail is about twice the length of the body and has a drawn out tip. The body is dark grayish brown with darker crossbands at the rear extending on to the base of the tail. Total length reaches 30 mm.

Habits and habitat: This species lives in primary or old secondary forest at low elevations. It has been found in peat swamps and in well-

W.M. Poon

Fig. 101. *Rhacophorus appendiculatus* (Günther).

drained forests. Males form large calling groups around low marshy areas or at slight depressions in the forest floor before any rain water has accumulated. The males perch on twigs and leaves of small trees one to three metres above ground. The tadpoles develop in these shallow bodies of standing water.

Call: A short to long series of soft clicking notes.

Distribution: Found throughout Borneo in appropriate environments. This species also occurs in Peninsular Malaysia, Sumatra, and the Philippine Islands.

Rhacophorus baluensis Inger
Kinabalu Tree Frog (Fig. 102)

Description: A medium-sized tree frog with a short, pointed snout. The toes are webbed to the base of the pads. The outer fingers are half-webbed and the inner ones a little less so. The skin of the top of the head and back is smooth or finely pebbled. The belly is coarsely pebbled. There is a smooth ridge of skin running from along the outerfinger along the edge of the forearm to the elbow and another one from along the outer toe along the lower leg to the heel. The heel itself has a distinct pointed skin flap. This species is variable in colouration and it is possible that an individual may change colour depending on temperature and light. The head and body are sandy beige to dark chocolate brown, with either dark transverse markings or irregular light blotches. There is a weak ridge of white bumps above the anus.
Males: 50–55 mm.
Females: 60–65 mm.

Tadpole: This is a large tadpole with an oval, slightly flattened body. The tail is shaped like an elongate leaf, with a blunt tip, and is about twice the body length. The colour is medium brown, slightly lighter below. Total length reaches 75 mm.

Habits and habitat: This frog lives in primary and disturbed forests at 1000–1500 metres above sea level. Males call in groups around small ponds, often at the edge of forests. All tadpoles have been found in these small ponds.

Fig. 102. *Rhacophorus baluensis* Inger.

Call: A deep rattle.

Distribution: Known only from the mountains of western Sabah and northeastern Sarawak.

Rhacophorus bimaculatus (Peters)
Blue-Spotted Tree Frog (Fig. 103)

Description: A small tree frog with a large eye and a pure white spot on the lip below the eye. (*Rhacophorus gauni* also has a white spot at that point.) The webbing reaches the base of the pads on all toes except the fourth. The two outer fingers are about half to two-thirds webbed and the inner fingers less webbed. The eye is about as large as the snout. The skin is smooth above and coarsely pebbled below. There is a narrow fringe along the edges of the outer finger and toe. Some frogs have several bumps along the edge of the forearm. The colour is medium to dark brown on the head and back with a darker bar between the eyes and usually one or two crossbars on the back. The sides are black with a number bright light blue spots; usually the top of the inner toes and webbing have the same pattern.

Males: 28–35 mm.
Females: 34–43 mm.

Tadpole: Unknown.

Habits and habitat: This species has been seen only in primary forests at low elevations. It has been found in flat and hilly forest. Although tadpoles have not been identified with certainty, they probably develop in riffles of clear streams since that is the environment where adults have always been collected.

Call: Unknown.

R.F. Inger

Fig. 103. *Rhacophorus bimaculatus* (Peters).

Distribution: Known from Kalimantan, Sabah, and Sarawak. It probably will be found in Brunei. Elsewhere it occurs in southern Thailand, Peninsular Malaysia, and the southern Philippines.

Rhacophorus dulitensis Boulenger
Jade Tree Frog (Fig. 104)

Dscription: A small tree frog with a sharply pointed snout and a slender body. The toes are webbed to the base of the pads. The fingers are almost fully webbed. The skin of the back is smooth. There is a narrow, white-edged ridge of skin along the outer edge of the forearm and another along the lower leg. The heel has a small conical or round flap of skin. A transverse ridge of skin projects above the anus. The entire upper surface of this frog is pale jade green with or without tiny white dots. The upper eyelid and a narrow line along the edge of the snout are reddish brown to purple. The top of the web between the outer toes is red. One of the oddities of this species is that the limb bones are turquoise green and visible through the flesh from the underside.

Males: 33–40 mm.

Females: 49–50 mm.

R.B. Stuebing

Fig. 104. *Rhacophorus dulitensis* Boulenger.

Tadpole: A large tadpole, with heavy, oval body. The tail is moderately deep and a little less than twice the body length. The body and front half of the tail are pale grayish brown. A wavy, black, vertical line crosses the tail at mid-length, beyond which the tail is darker. Total length reaches 50 mm.

Habits and habitat: This is a frog of primary lowland forest in flat or hilly country in the lowlands. Little is known of its habits. It forms large breeding groups around forest ponds at unpredictable intervals, apparently stimulated by sudden heavy rains. The tadpoles live in these ponds.

Call: A short, weak, cricket-like trill.

Distribution: Known from Sabah and Sarawak. It probably will be found in Brunei and Kalimantan. It also occurs in Sumatra.

Rhacophorus everetti Boulenger
Mossy Tree Frog (Fig. 105)

Description: A small stocky frog, with slender, long legs and a short, blunt snout. The webbing on the toes does not quite reach the base of the pads. The fingers are webbed only at the bases. The skin of the upper surfaces is rough, with many tiny pointed projections over the head and back. There is a semicircle of spikey projection running over the shoulders between the eardrums and numerous similar, though smaller, projections scattered over the back. The forearm and lower leg have a row of cone-shaped projections along the outer edge. These frogs are mottled in colours from light green to dark brown. The top of the head is dark, with a light bar between the eyes. The back is a mixture of patches of tan and brown. The upper thighs are usually greenish yellow with brown spots. The underside of the legs are green.
Males 30–32 mm.
Females: 45–49 mm.

Tadpole: Unknown.

Habits and habitat: This frog lives in primary submontane and montane forests from 1100 to 1800 metres above sea level. It is often found in mossy areas, as on fallen logs near streams. Little is known of its habits.

Call: Unknown.

Distribution: Mountains of western Sabah and northeastern Sarawak. Also known from Palawan in the Philippine Islands.

Fig. 105. *Rhacophorus everetti* Boulenger.

Rhacophorus gauni (Inger)
Short-Nosed Tree Frog (Fig. 106)

Description: A small slender-bodied tree frog with a very short snout and prominent, bulging eyes. All toes except the fourth webbed to the base of the pads. The outer fingers are almost fully webbed. The upper surfaces of the body are smooth, though there usually is a small, sharply pointed, vertical projection near the edge of the upper eyelid. There is also a small pointed projection at the heel and three or four others between the heel and the base of the outer toe. The back is usually light

186

tan with several large dark spots. There is a conspicuous white spot below the eye. The hidden surfaces of the thighs are a rich golden yellow.

Males: 26–30 mm.

Females: 35–38 mm.

Tadpole: This small tadpole has an oval body distinctly flattened below, and a broadly rounded snout. The tail is slender, tapering to a rounded tip, and is almost twice the body length. The mouth is surrounded by wide lips that hang down forming a cup-like structure. The beaks are black, thick and V-shaped. The body is yellowish brown. The tail muscle has brown or black spots. Total length reaches 25 mm.

Fig. 106. *Rhacophorus gauni* (Inger).

Habits and habitat: This species lives in primary forest in hilly country from near sea level to 750 metres. It lives in vegetation overhanging the riffles of clear, rocky streams. Calling males form loose groups. Females attach their white foam nest to leaves overhanging the stream. The small, slender tadpoles move into riffles and live in the crevices among the gravel and rocks of the bottom.

187

Call: A single sharp note, a high-pitched chirp.

Distribution: Known from Sabah and Sarawak.

Rhacophorus harrissoni Inger & Haile
Brown Tree Frog (Fig. 107)

Description: A medium-sized tree frog with a pointed, sharp-edged snout. All of the toes are broadly webbed to the base of the pads. The three out fingers are also webbed to the pads. The skin of the back is finely pebbled or smooth. The belly is coarsely pebbled. There are no ridges or flaps of skin on the limbs. The head and back of this rather plain frog are reddish brown or clay brown. The side of the head sometimes has white spots. The sides and the hidden surfaces of the legs are greenish yellow. The webbing of the fingers and toes is dark brown or black.
Males: 50–56mm.
Females: 60–70 mm.

Fig. 107. *Rhacophorus harrissoni* Inger & Haile.

Tadpole: The body is oval, generally rounded above and below. The tail is about twice the body length. The body and tail are dark gray. Total length reaches 41 mm.

Habits and habitat: This species has been found in primary and old secondary forests in hilly country at low elevations. Little is known about the usual foraging height of this species, but it descends to within a few metres of the ground to breed. All tadpoles known have been observed in water within tree "holes" 1–4 metres above ground. Foam nests have been seen attached to bark just above a tree hole. Some of these tadpole sites were holes in tree trunks; others were formed by the fusing of trunk buttresses making rather large tanks.

Call: Unknown.

Distribution: Known from Sabah and Sarawak.

Rhacophorus kajau Dring
White-Eared Tree Frog (Fig. 108)

Description: A very small tree frog, with outer fingers only about one-third webbed. Toes are about half-webbed. The skin is finely pebbled on the back and coarsely pebbled on the belly. A narrow, wavy ridge of skin runs along the outer finger and outer edge of the forearm and a similar ridge runs along the outer toe and edge of the lower leg. There is a narrow transverse ridge below the anus. The colour is leafy green on all upper surfaces, usually with minute white spots scattered over the back, head, and exposed surfaces of the limbs. The eardrum and the inner fingers are white. The lower sides and belly are without pigment. The webbing is black and the hidden surfaces of the thigh have an orange tinge.
Males: 18–20 mm.
Females: Unknown.

Tadpole: The body is oval and rounded. The tail is drawn out into a narrow tip and is about twice the body length. A large brown blotch covers most of the top and sides of the body. The tail muscle has brown spots, but is mostly pale. Total length reaches 17 mm.

Habits and habitat: This is a poorly known species that has been seen only a few times. It lives, so far as we know, only in primary forest at low elevations. Males have been found on leaves of shrubs and small trees overhanging small, slowly flowing intermittent streams and marshes.

Call: A series of single or double clicks made at intervals.

Distribution: Sabah and Sarawak.

Fig. 108. *Rhacophorus kajau* Dring.

Rhacophorus nigropalmatus Boulenger
Wallace's Flying Frog (Fig. 109)

Description: A very large tree frog with an almost rounded snout and very large large hands and feet. Fingers and toes are fully webbed. The skin of the body is very finely pebbled, but has no projections or ridges. The forearm has a wide, smooth-edged flap of skin that extends to the edge of the outer finger. The heel has a wide, rounded flap of skin that continues onto the outer edge of the foot. All upper surfaces are emerald green, sometimes with a few glossy white spots on the back. The underside is white, becoming yellowish on the chest and belly. The sides of the body and legs are deep yellow. The webbing of the feet is black, fading into yellow towards the tips of the toes.

Males: 79–89 mm.

Females: 89–100 mm.

Tadpole: The body is oval and rounded. The tail is a bit less than twice the body length and is rather deep. The body is pale gray above and white below. The tail has black spots on the muscle and fins, with a dark edge to the upper fin. Total length reaches 50 mm.

Habits and habitat: This is the original "Flying Frog of Borneo." It is a resident of primary forest at low elevations. Frogs come down from the forest canopy to breed at turbid pools of water, and form small groups around wild pig or rhino wallows. Large foam nests are attached either

R.F. Inger

Fig. 109. *Rhacophorus nigropalmatus* Boulenger.

191

to mud banks or vegetation overhanging the pools. The tadpoles often develop in extremely murky, turbid water.

Call: Not described.

Distribution: Known from Kalimantan, Sabah, and Sarawak. It undoubtedly occurs in Brunei. The species has also been found in southern Thailand, Peninsular Malaysia, and Sumatra.

Rhacophorus pardalis Günther
Harlequin Tree Frog (Fig. 110)

Description: This is a small to medium-sized tree frog, with a rounded snout. The toes and the three outer fingers are fully webbed to the pads. The skin of the back is smooth, while the belly is coarsely pebbled. A wide smooth-edged flap of skin runs along the outer edge of the foarearm and hand. The heel has a rounded flap of skin.

The upper surfaces are tan to reddish brown, with dark markings often forming an X in the middle of the back. Most individuals have several white spots on the back and some have yellow or blue spots on the back and upper surfaces of the legs. The sides and belly are yellowish, with black spots on the sides and an orange network on the belly. The webbing on hands and feet is orange-red.
Males: 39–55 mm.
Females: 55–71 mm.

Tadpole: The body is oval and rather deep. The tail is slightly less than twice the body length and tapers to a narrow tip. The body is pale light brown. Some tadpoles have several black spots on the body, while others have just one spot on the side of the head. Total length reaches 45 mm. These tadpoles may be confused with those of *Rana chalconota* because of their spotted pattern, but only the latter have white glandular patches on the underside.

Habits and habitat: This frog, which is a proficient glider, is found in a wide variety of forested habitats at low elevations. It forms small breeding groups around marshes, ponds, and quiet side pools of streams.

Fig. 110. *Rhacophorus pardalis* Günther.

It is relatively common along logging roads where streams are often blocked and form pools. The normal foraging habitat is unknown, but is presumably in the forest canopy. The tadpoles develop in standing water.

Call: A brief raspy chuckle.

Distribution: Known from Kalimantan, Sabah, and Sarawak. It will probably be found in Brunei. It also occurs in Sumatra and the southern Philippine Islands.

Rhacophorus reinwardti (Schlegel)
Reinwardt's Flying Frog (Fig. 5 & 111)

Description: A medium-sized to large tree frog with a broad head. The toes and three outer fingers are fully webbed to the pads. The skin is granular, more coarsely on the sides and belly. The outer edge of the forearm has a wide, smooth-edged flap of skin. The heel has a wide, rounded flap, continuing as a narrow strip along the edge of the lower leg. The upper surfaces are a rich, dark green, fading into golden yellow towards the sides. The sides have a black band set with turquoise blue spots. In some frogs the the back is limited to small areas surrounding the blue spots. The webbingis black with golden yellow and light blue spots. The throat, chest, and belly are pure white.
Males: 46–55 mm.
Females: 56–65 mm.

Tadpole: Unknown.

Habits and habitat: This handsome frog has been found only in primary forests at low elevations. It descends from the canopy to breed around semi-permaent pools on the forest floor. As this species has been found only a few times in Borneo, little is known of its habits. Adults probably feed on canopy insects.

Call: A low crackling chuckle.

Distribution: Known from Sabah and Sarawak. It also occurs in Java, Sumatra, and Peninsular Malaysia.

Fig. 111. *Rhacophorus reinwardti* (Schlegel).

Rhacophorus rufipes Inger
Red-Legged Tree Frog (Fig. 112)

Description: This is a small tree frog with triangular, pointed head. The toes are fully webbed. The outer fingers are also extensively webbed, but the web does not quite reach the pads. The skin is smooth on the upper surfaces, but coarsely granular on the belly. There are no fringes or flaps of skin on the limbs. The colour of the upper surfaces is tan to reddish brown with a few brown spots or cross bands. The webbing of the hands and feet and the hidden surfaces of the legs are bright orange-red. The underside of the body is pale yellowish without the orange network seen in *R. pardalis*.
Males: 33–39 mm.
Females: 48–50 mm.

195

Tadpole: Unknown.

Habits and habitat: Little is known about this species. It has been found only in primary forest at low elevations. It forms breeding groups on vegetation within two metres of the ground. It seems to breed in short, unpredictable bursts, subsequently disappearing. Nothing is known of the normal foraging area of this species.

Call: Unknown.

Distribution: Known so far only from Sabah and Sarawak.

R.F. Inger

Fig. 112. *Rhacophorus rufipes* Inger.

Further Reading

Berry, P.Y. 1975. *The Amphibian Fauna of Peninsular Malaysia.* Tropical Press, Kuala Lumpur. x + 130 pp.

Campbell, E.J.F. 1994. *A Walk through the Lowland Rain Forest of Sabah.* Natural History Publications (Borneo) Sdn. Bhd., Kota Kinabalu. viii + 83 pp.

Inger, R.F. 1990. *The Systematics and Zoogeography of the Amphibia of Borneo. Fieldiana: Zoology* 52: 1–402. (2nd printing)

Inger, R.F. & R.B. Stuebing. 1989. *Frogs of Sabah.* Sabah Parks Publication no. 10. Sabah Parks Trustees, Kota Kinabalu. iv + 133 pp.

Inger, R.F. & R.B. Stuebing. 1992. *The Montane Amphibian fauna of Northwestern Borneo. Malayan Nature Journal* 46: 1–51.

Inger, R.F., R.B. Stuebing & Tan Fui Lian. 1995. *New species and new records of Anurans from Borneo. The Raffles Bulletin of Zoology (Singapore)* 43(1): 115–131.

Inger, R.F, R.B. Stuebing & Tan Fui Lian. 1996. **Frogs and Toads**, in: *Kinabalu—Summit of Borneo* (2nd edition) (eds. Wong, K.M. & A. Phillipps). Sabah Society Monograph. The Sabah Society, Kota Kinabalu. pp. 353–367.

Wong, Anna. 1994. *Population Ecology of Amphibians in Different Altitudes of Kinabalu Park. Sabah Museum Journal* 1(2): 29–38

Wong, K.M. & C.L. Chan. 1997. *Mount Kinabalu—Borneo's Magic Mountain.* Natural History Publications (Borneo) Sdn. Bhd., Kota Kinabalu. viii + 95 pp.

Yates, S. 1992. *The Nature of Borneo.* Facts On File, New York. xvi + 208 pp.

Acknowledgements

We greatly appreciate the Foreword prepared by Y.B. Datuk Tham Nyip Shen, Deputy Chief Minister and Minister of Industrial Devlopment, Sabah, and for his general encouragement of natural science in Sabah. Support of our field work in Borneo came from Field Museum of Natural History (Chicago), International Tropical Timber Organization, and John D. and Catherine T. MacArthur Foundation. We received much logistical support from Datuk Lamri Ali, Director, and Mr. Francis Liew, Deputy Director, Sabah Parks; Prof. Ghazally Ismail, formerly of Universiti Kebangsaan Malaysia (Sabah Campus); Mr. Cheong Ek Choon and Mr. James Dawos Mamit of Forestry Department, Sarawak; Dr. Charles Leh, Sarawak Museum; and staff of Sabah Forest Industries. We thank C.L. Chan, Arthur Y.C. Chung, Hans Hazebroek, Maurice Kottelat, Kelvin Lim, Stephen Von Peltz, and W. M. Poon for use of their photographs and Tan Fui Lian for use of her drawings. Our work in the field would not have been possible or pleasurable without the help and association of Tan Fui Lian, Alim Biun, Paul Yambun, Danson Kandong, Freddy Paulus, Frederick Francis, Patrick Francis, Anna Wong, Albert Lo, Shahbuddin Hj Sabky, Saifuddin Senawi and Taib Jainudin. Our work in the laboratory was greatly assisted by Mr. Alan Resetar and Ms. Cassandra Redhed. Mervin Chin and Jacky Chua Kok Hian assisted with the layout. We are very grateful to all of these persons and organizations.

Index

202

V

W

205

Other titles available through *Natural History Publications:*

Mount Kinabalu: Borneo's Magic Moutain—an introduction to the natural history of one of the world's great natural monuments *by* K.M. Wong & C.L. Chan

Kinabalu: Summit of Borneo (*eds.* K.M. Wong & A. Phillipps)

Kinabalu: The Haunted Mountain of Borneo *by* C.M. Enriquez (Reprint)

A Colour Guide to Kinabalu Park *by* S.K. Jacobson

Parks of Sabah *by* A. Phillipps

The Larger Fungi of Borneo *by* D.N. Pegler

Pitcher-plants of Borneo *by* A. Phillipps & A. Lamb

Nepenthes of Borneo *by* C. Clarke

Rafflesia: Magnificent Flower of Sabah *by* Kamarudin Mat Salleh

Tree Flora of Sabah and Sarawak Vol. 1 (*eds.* E. Soepadmo & K.M. Wong)

Tree Flora of Sabah and Sarawak Vol. 2. (*eds.* E. Soepadmo, K.M. Wong & L.G. Saw)

Trees of Sabah Vol. 1 *by* P.F. Cockburn

Trees of Sabah Vol. 2 *by* P.F. Cockburn

Dipterocarps of Sabah *by* W. Meijer & J. Wood

The Morphology, Anatomy, Biology and Classification of Peninsular Malaysian Bamboos *by* K.M. Wong

The Bamboos of Peninsular Malaysia *by* K.M. Wong

The Bamboos of Sabah *by* S. Dransfield

Rattans of Sabah *by* J. Dransfield

The Plants of Mount Kinabalu 1: Ferns *by* B.S. Parris *et al.*

The Plants of Mount Kinabalu 2: Orchids *by* J.J. Wood *et al.*

Orchids of Borneo Vol.1 *by* C.L. Chan *et al.*

Orchids of Borneo Vol. 2 *by* J.J. Vermeulen

Orchids of Borneo Vol. 3 *by* J.J. Wood

A Checklist of the Orchids of Borneo *by* P.J. Cribb & J.J. Wood

Slipper Orchids of Borneo *by* P.J. Cribb

Orchids of Java *by* J.B. Comber

Flowers and Plants of Mount Kinabalu *by* T. Sato

Mosses and Liverworts of Mount Kinabalu *by* Frahm *et al.*

Birds of Mount Kinabalu, Borneo *by* G.W.H. Davison

Proboscis Monkeys of Borneo *by* E.L. Bennett & F. Gombek

The Natural History of Orang-utan *by* E.L. Bennett

A Field Guide to the Mammals of Borneo *by* J. Payne *et al.*

Checklist of Lizards of Sabah *by* Tan Fui Lian

The Systematics and Zoogeography of the Amphibia of Borneo *by* R.F. Inger (Reprint)

The Natural History of Amphibians and Reptiles in Sabah *by* R.F. Inger & Tan Fui Lian

Pocket Guide to the Birds of Borneo *by* C.M. Francis

Birds of Pelong Rocks *by* M. Wong & Hj. Mohammad bin Hj. Ibrahim

The Fresh-water Fishes of North Borneo *by* R.F. Inger & P.K. Chin

Termites of Sabah *by* R.S. Thapa

Forest Pest Insects in Sabah *by* V.K. Chey

Common Seashore Life of Brunei *by* M. Wong & Aziah binte Hj. Ahmad

Common Lowland Rainforest Ants of Sabah *by* Arthur Chung

Borneo: the Stealer of Hearts *by* O. Cooke (Reprint)

Land Below the Wind *by* A. Keith (Reprint)

A Sabah Gazetteer *by* J. Tangah & K.M. Wong

In Brunei Forests: An Introduction to the Plant Life of Brunei Darussalam *by* K.M. Wong (Revised edition)

A Walk through the Lowland Rainforest of Sabah *by* E.J.F. Campbell

Manual latihan pemuliharaan dan penyelidikan hidupan liar di lapangan *by* A. Rabinowitz (*Translated by* Maryati Mohamad)

Enchanted Gardens of Kinabalu: A Borneo Diary *by* S.M. Phillipps

The Theory and Application of a Systems Approach to Silvicultural Decision-making *by* M. Kleine

Dipsim: A Dipterocarp Forest Growth Simulation Model for Sabah *by* R. Ong & M. Kleine

Kadazan Dusun–Malay–English Dictionary (*eds.* R. Lasimbang *et al.*)

An Introduction to the Traditional Costumes of Sabah (*eds.* R. Lasimbang & S. Moo-Tan)